ESCOFFIER KITCHEN HANDBOOKS

STOCKS, SAUCES
&
GARNISHES

ESCOFFIER KITCHEN HANDBOOKS

STOCKS, SAUCES
&
GARNISHES

Selected and Edited by
Hilary Newstead

CONSULTANT EDITORS
H.L.CRACKNELL & R.J.KAUFMANN

THE KINGSWOOD PRESS

The Kingswood Press
an imprint of William Heinemann Limited
10 Upper Grosvenor Street
London W1X 9PA

LONDON   MELBOURNE
JOHANNESBURG   AUCKLAND

Adapted from:
The Complete Guide to the Art of Modern Cookery
by A.Escoffier
translated by H.L.Cracknell and R.J.Kaufmann
(London: Heinemann, 1979)

Printed in Spain

ISBN 0 434 23902 X

Acknowledgements
Editors Andrew Jefford, Norma MacMillan
Art Editor Alyson Kyles
Production Shane Lask

Illustrations by Christine Robins/The Garden Studio

NOTES

1. Metric and imperial measurements have been calculated
separately, and are approximate rather than exact equivalents.
Therefore use only one set of measurements, either metric or
imperial, when preparing the recipes.

2. Words printed in *italics* in the recipes indicate that the word is
included in the short Glossary on page 109.

CONTENTS

INTRODUCTION

A glossy, satin-smooth sauce, rich in aroma and taste, can transform an everyday dish into the realms of gastronomic delight. In their pleasing shades of chestnut brown, shell pink, soft green or creamy white, sauces can be used to good effect as decoration; it is the perfect taste, though, which should be striven for above all.

Sauces should enhance the main item of food, not over-power it or mask its own particular flavour. They should bring a complementary range of tastes to this main item, to whet the appetite, excite the palate and aid digestion.

Originally designed and created for use in hotels and restaurants, these sauces respect the detail of Escoffier's original recipes. They have, though, been redrafted specifically for use in the home kitchen.

Also included in this book are descriptions of the classic garnishes in which so many of the sauces found their place in Escoffier's day. They enable the keen reader to recreate some of the splendour of classic French cooking.

BASIC
PREPARATIONS

Les Fonds de Cuisine

*B*efore the sauce – the stock. In most cases, it is only by the use of high quality – and appropriate – stocks that perfect sauces can be achieved. Most of us are aware of the importance given by hotels and catering establishments to their stockpots continually bubbling away in the background. The length of time and quantities involved in stock making often daunt the home cook, and commercial stock cubes and seasonings are consequently much used. Yet the same cook is prepared to spend great time and care over all other aspects of the special meal or dinner party. It seems to be a question of overcoming this reluctance – just once, because having tasted a traditionally made sauce no one would dispute that the end amply justifies the means.

Fonds Brun

1.5 kg (3 lb 6 oz) shin of beef, on the bone
1.5 kg (3 lb 6 oz) knuckle of veal or lean veal trimmings
150 g (5 oz) carrot, peeled and roughly chopped
150 g (5 oz) onion, peeled and roughly chopped
6 tablespoons clean fat, such as strained dripping
1 knuckle raw ham, blanched
150 g (5 oz) fresh pork rind, blanched
1 bouquet garni
4.5 litres (8 pints) water

*B*one the beef and veal, break the bones up small and lightly brown them in the oven. Fry the carrot and onion in half the fat until nicely browned.

Place the bones, vegetables, ham, pork rind and bouquet garni in a stockpot, then add the cold water. Bring to the boil, skim and simmer very gently for at least 12 hours, adding water as required to maintain the liquid level throughout.

Cut the beef and veal meat into large dice, heat the remaining fat and fry until brown. Place in a pan, cover with some of the prepared stock and boil until reduced to a glaze. Repeat this process 2 or 3 times. Add the rest of the prepared stock, bring to the boil, skim to remove all fat, and allow to simmer gently until all the flavour has been extracted from the meat; maintain the level of the liquid with water as required.

Strain and reserve for use.

Uses

This excellent recipe makes a general purpose brown stock suitable for use in many sauces, soups and stews, and for braising. Fonds Brun may be frozen in manageable quantities for domestic use.

MAKES APPROXIMATELY 2.5 LITRES ($4\frac{1}{2}$ PINTS)

Fonds Blanc

1.5 kg (3 lb 6 oz) shin of veal, veal trimmings and veal bones
4 raw chicken carcasses, with giblets
1 teaspoon salt
125 g (4½ oz) carrot, peeled and roughly chopped
65 g (2½ oz) onion, peeled and roughly chopped
50 g (2 oz) leek, chopped
15 g (½ oz) celery, chopped
1 bouquet garni

*B*one the shin and chop the bones very small. Place all the bones and meat in a stockpot, cover well with cold water and add the salt. Bring to the boil, skim carefully and add the vegetables and bouquet garni. Allow to simmer gently, uncovered, for 3 hours, removing scum and fat and adding boiling water as required to keep the liquid to the same level for half the cooking time. Add no more liquid thereafter. Strain and reserve for use.

Uses

This is a good general purpose stock which should be used as the poaching medium and foundation for the final sauces in all blanquette dishes, and veal and chicken fricassées. Fonds Blanc also provides the base for Sauce Tomate, page 31, and Sauce Allemande, page 53.

Variation

Fonds Blanc de Volaille, necessary for Sauces Velouté de Volaille, page 28, and Suprême, page 29, is made as above, but with more chicken in proportion to veal. This can be achieved by using more giblets or carcass, or by using a whole, quartered boiling fowl in place of an equal weight of veal.

MAKES APPROXIMATELY 1.5 LITRES (2½ PINTS)

Fonds Brun de Veau

1.25 kg (2½ lb) boned shin or shoulder of veal
1 tablespoon dripping
1 kg (2¼ lb) veal bones, chopped into small pieces
150 g (5 oz) carrot, peeled and sliced
90 g (3½ oz) onion, peeled and sliced
1 small bay leaf
1 small sprig thyme
3 parsley stalks
4 litres (7 pints) Fonds Blanc, page 10

Roll and tie the shin or shoulder of veal, brush with the dripping, season and brown in the oven with the bones. Cover the bottom of a stockpot with the vegetables, then add the herbs, meat and bones. Cover the pan and set over a gentle heat to cook for 10 minutes. Moisten with 300 ml (½ pint) of stock and cook rapidly to reduce to a glaze. Repeat this process 2 more times. Add the remaining stock, bring to the boil and simmer gently for 4–5 hours. Skim frequently, and add more stock or water if necessary to maintain a liquid level of 2 litres (3½ pints). Strain and reserve for use.

Uses
When thickened, Fonds Brun de Veau gives the delicious veal gravy known as Jus de Veau Lié, page 25. This can be served on its own with grilled steaks, lamb and veal cutlets and omelettes, and is also used as the base for certain brown sauces. Fonds Brun de Veau may be used in place of Fonds Brun, page 9, where a more pronounced veal flavour is required.

Variation
A similar veal stock may be made using water instead of Fonds Blanc, in which case 2 teaspoons salt should also be added.
MAKES APPROXIMATELY 2 LITRES (3½ PINTS)

Fonds de Gibier

1 kg (2 lb) game, to include a variety selected from rabbit,
pheasant, venison or hare, preferably older animals and birds,
but fresh
75 g (3 oz) carrot, peeled and sliced
75 g (3 oz) green of leek, sliced
75 g (3 oz) onion, peeled and sliced
40 g (1½ oz) celery, sliced
65 g (2½ oz) mushrooms, sliced, or mushroom trimmings
25 g (1 oz) butter
1 clove garlic
15 g (½ oz) parsley stalks
1 pinch chopped fresh thyme
1 bay leaf
good pinch salt
15 juniper berries and 1 clove, tied together in muslin

*C*ut the game into pieces and brown in a hot oven (220°C,
425°F, Gas Mark 7). Place the vegetables in the bottom of a
heavy pan and fry until brown in the butter with all the
flavouring ingredients except the juniper and clove. Add the
browned pieces of game.

Deglaze the roasting pan with a little water and add the other
ingredients. Cover all with water, add the juniper and clove and
bring to the boil. Skim carefully. Allow to simmer very gently,
skimming as and when necessary, for 3 hours, maintaining the
level of the liquid with water as required.

Strain and reserve for use.

Uses

Fonds de Gibier provides the foundation for brown game
sauces, the most notable of which is Sauce Poivrade for Game,
page 46. It may also be reduced and thickened with arrowroot
to make a sauce suitable for serving with roast saddle of venison.

MAKES APPROXIMATELY 1.5 LITRES (2½ PINTS)

Fumet de Poisson

1.5 kg (3 lb 6 oz) bones and trimmings of sole, whiting or brill
65 g (2½ oz) onion, peeled and sliced
40 g (1½ oz) white of mushroom, chopped
1 pinch salt
a few parsley stalks
1.5 litres (2½ pints) water
½ bottle good dry white wine
a few drops lemon juice
5 peppercorns

*P*ut the fish bones and trimmings, onion, mushroom, salt and parsley stalks into a pan and cover with the water. Add the wine and lemon juice. Bring to the boil quickly, skim and allow to simmer very gently for 20 minutes. Add the peppercorns and continue cooking for 10 more minutes.

Strain and reserve for use.

Uses

This stock is used in the preparation of fish sauces, and as a poaching medium for white fish.

MAKES APPROXIMATELY 1.5 LITRES (2½ PINTS)

Roux

Roux are used as thickening agents for basic sauces: Roux Blanc for Sauce Béchamel and other white sauces, Roux Blond for various Velouté and cream sauces, and Roux Brun for brown sauces. To ensure that perfectly smooth sauces are obtained allow the roux to cool before gradually adding the hot liquid whilst stirring continuously.

Roux Blanc and Blond should be made as and when required, whereas Roux Brun may be made in advance if necessary. The following methods are ideal for domestic purposes where the quantities of fat and flour are unlikely to exceed 100–150 g (4–5 oz). If larger quantities of roux are called for, the ingredients should be mixed in a heavy pan over a gentle heat then transferred to a moderate oven (160°–180°C, 325°–350°F, Gas Mark 3–4) and cooked until the appropriate colour is achieved.

Clarified butter is necessary for the preparation of roux. To clarify butter, place the required amount in a deep, narrow pan and stand in a container of hot water to melt and settle for half an hour. Carefully remove any scum from the top, then strain off the clear butter fat without disturbing the sediment.

Roux Blanc
Use approximately 5 parts of clarified butter to 6 parts of plain flour. Melt the butter in a pan, draw off the heat and stir in the flour. Cook over a gentle heat, stirring continuously, to eliminate the flavour of uncooked flour but taking care that the mixture does not colour.

Roux Blond
Use the same ingredients and method as for Roux Blanc but continue to cook until the mixture colours to a pale straw.

Roux Brun
Use the same ingredients and method as for Roux Blanc but continue to cook the mixture, stirring frequently, until it is light brown, perfectly smooth and smells of baked flour.

Liaisons

Liaisons are thickening or binding agents designed to give body and consistency to flavoured liquids such as sauces, and to form them into homogenous mixtures.

Beurre Manié

This butter is used as a quick thickening for sauces. It is made by mixing butter and flour together to a smooth paste in the proportions of 75 g (3 oz) flour to 100 g (4 oz) butter. The sauce under preparation should be brought to the boil then allowed to simmer whilst stirring or whisking in small knobs of the butter until the correct consistency is achieved.

Cooked mixtures of flour and butter, also used as thickening agents for sauces, are called roux and are described opposite.

Fécules

Fécules or starch solutions may be used to thicken soups and sauces. Cornflour, arrowroot, rice flour and potato flour may be used as appropriate. Small quantities of the starch should be mixed with cold water or liquid and stirred into the boiling soup or sauce. Continue to stir and allow to simmer for a few minutes until the thickening has taken place and the starch is cooked.

Egg and Cream Liaisons

Egg yolks and cream may be whisked together and used to thicken delicate soups and sauces. Use 1 egg yolk and 50 ml (2 fl oz) cream per 500 ml (18 fl oz) of liquid. Remove the soup or sauce from the heat and stir in the liaison. Stir over a gentle heat until the thickening has been effected, taking care that the mixture does not boil.

Glace de Viande

2.5 litres (4½ pints) Fonds Brun, page 9

*P*lace the stock in a large pan and cook until it has reduced by three-quarters of its original volume. Strain into a smaller pan, lower the heat and allow to simmer gently and further reduce. Skim the stock carefully and frequently to remove any scum. The glaze is ready when it coats the back of a spoon and is glossy in appearance. Transfer to a small bowl, cover and refrigerate until needed. It is best used within one week of making. Alternatively, the glaze may be spooned into ice-cube trays and frozen until required.

Uses
Appropriate glazes can be added to light and brown sauces to give them extra strength, colour and brilliance. Glace de Viande can be used to brush on to grilled steaks, and when finished with butter makes a good accompaniment to grilled lamb cutlets. Roll noisette potatoes in melted Glace de Viande, and serve with artichoke bottoms and Sauce Béarnaise, page 55, to form the '*Henri IV*' garnish for tournedos.

Variations
A lighter coloured, clear meat glaze is made by substituting Fonds Blanc, page 10, for the Fonds Brun. Delicate threads of light meat glaze can be drawn over some finished dishes, such as poached calves' brains, for decoration. *Glace de Volaille* and *Glace de Poisson* are made in the above manner using Fonds Blanc de Volaille, page 10, and Fumet de Poisson, page 13.
MAKES APPROXIMATELY 50 ML (2 FL OZ)

Cuisson de Champignons

450 g (1 lb) white mushrooms, finely chopped
juice of $\frac{1}{4}$ lemon
25 g (1 oz) butter
1 pinch salt
50 ml (2 fl oz) water

*P*lace the mushrooms in a pan with the lemon juice, butter, salt and water. Cover, heat slowly and simmer for a few minutes only. Squeeze firmly through muslin or a very fine strainer to extract all the liquid.

Uses
This is a very useful flavouring agent for a wide variety of sauces.

Variations
Essence de Champignons is made by reducing Cuisson de Champignons over a gentle heat by about half.

For **Essence de Truffes**, take peelings and trimmings of truffles and cover with Madeira or port wine. Bring to the boil, then allow to infuse until cold. Strain and reserve for use. Black truffles from Périgord are the best for this purpose.

MAKES APPROXIMATELY 150 ML ($\frac{1}{4}$ PINT)

Essence de Poisson

100 g (4 oz) butter
150 g (5 oz) onion, peeled and sliced
350 g (12 oz) mushroom trimmings
50 g (2 oz) parsley stalks
1.75 kg (4 lb) head, bones and trimmings of whiting or sole
300 ml ($\frac{1}{2}$ pint) good dry white wine
juice of 1 lemon
1.5 litres (2$\frac{1}{2}$ pints) Fumet de Poisson, page 13
1 pinch salt

*M*elt the butter in a large pan and add the onion, mushroom trimmings and parsley stalks. Cook until the onion is softened but not coloured. Add the fish bones and trimmings, cover and stew for 15 minutes, moving the ingredients occasionally. Pour in the wine and reduce by half, then add the lemon juice, Fumet de Poisson and salt. Bring to the boil and allow to simmer gently for 15 minutes only. Carefully skim the surface, then strain and reserve for use.

Uses
This is a concentrated form of Fumet de Poisson used primarily in the poaching of flat fish, particularly sole and turbot. The essence imparts extra flavour, and is usually reduced and added to the accompanying sauce. Alternatively, the cooking liquor can be reduced and finished with a little butter to give a glossy sauce with which to coat the fish.

Variation
Glace de Poisson, like other glazes, is made by steadily reducing stock (in this case Fumet de Poisson) until a syrupy coating consistency is reached (see page 16). However, in practice, Essence de Poisson provides a more delicate flavour and is generally to be preferred.

MAKES APPROXIMATELY 1 LITRE (1$\frac{3}{4}$ PINTS)

Essence de Tomate

750 g (1½ lb) very ripe tomatoes

Roughly chop the tomatoes and rub through a fine sieve. Discard the skin and pips and pour the juice into a small pan. Cook gently until it reduces to a syrupy consistency. Let the essence drip through muslin, without squeezing, and collect in a small bowl. Cover and refrigerate until needed.

Uses
Use this essence, which has a more delicate flavour than fresh or commercial tomato purée, to give extra flavour and colour to stuffings and certain brown sauces. It is most important in the making of **Jus Lié Tomaté**: add 150 ml (¼ pint) Essence de Tomate to 500 ml (18 fl oz) Fonds Brun de Veau, page 11, and reduce by one-fifth. Pass through a fine strainer and thicken with 15 g (½ oz) arrowroot mixed with a little cold water. Serve this tomato gravy with a wide variety of meats.

Variation
Another small preparation of tomatoes often used as a garnish or part of a dish is **Fondue de Tomate** or **Fondue Portugaise**: soften 50 g (2 oz) chopped onion in a little butter and add 250 g (9 oz) peeled, depipped and roughly chopped tomatoes, a small crushed clove of garlic and salt and pepper. Cook gently until the mixture is almost dry. If too acid, adjust the seasoning with a little caster sugar. Large grilled mushrooms are filled with well-reduced Fondue de Tomate for the '*à la Mexicaine*' garnish for cuts or joints of meat and poultry, together with grilled red peppers and Jus Lié Tomaté (see above).

MAKES APPROXIMATELY 65 ML (2½ FL OZ)

Court-bouillon au Vin Blanc

600 ml (1 pint) white wine
600 ml (1 pint) water
150 g (5 oz) onion, peeled and sliced
20 g ($\frac{3}{4}$ oz) parsley stalks
1 small sprig thyme
$\frac{1}{2}$ small bay leaf
15 g ($\frac{1}{2}$ oz) coarse salt
6 peppercorns

*P*lace all the ingredients except for the peppercorns in a pan, bring to the boil and simmer gently for 10 minutes. Then add the peppercorns and simmer for a further 10 minutes. Strain and reserve for use.

Uses

This is required in the making of **Sauce Matelote Blanche**: place 300 ml ($\frac{1}{2}$ pint) of the court-bouillon in a pan with 25 g (1 oz) mushroom trimmings; reduce by two-thirds. Add 750 ml (1$\frac{1}{4}$ pints) Velouté de Poisson, page 28; simmer for 5 minutes, then pass through a fine strainer. Finish with 150 g (5 oz) butter and a touch of cayenne pepper. Add 20 button onions, glazed in butter, and 20 cooked button mushrooms.

MAKES APPROXIMATELY 1 LITRE (1$\frac{3}{4}$ PINTS)

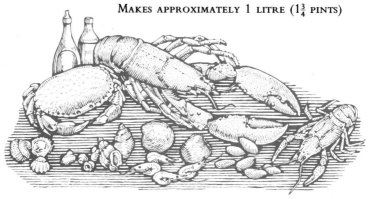

Court-bouillon au Vinaigre

1 litre (1¾ pints) water
50 ml (2 fl oz) white wine vinegar
10 g (⅓ oz) coarse salt
125 g (4½ oz) carrot, peeled and sliced
100 g (4 oz) onion, peeled and sliced
1 sprig thyme
½ bay leaf
20 g (¾ oz) parsley stalks
a few peppercorns

P lace all the ingredients in a pan except for the peppercorns. Bring to the boil and simmer gently for about 1 hour. Add the peppercorns 10 minutes before the end. Strain and reserve for use.

Uses

Both Court-bouillon au Vinaigre and Court-bouillon au Vin Blanc, opposite, can be used as the poaching liquor for whole and large cuts of salmon and trout. To poach a 1 kg (2¼ lb) piece of salmon or whole salmon trout, lay it in a fish kettle and cover with cold court-bouillon. Bring to the boil slowly, skim, then reduce the heat and allow to poach without any boiling of the liquid, for 10–12 minutes. Serve one or two of the following sauces with the salmon: Sauces aux Crevettes, page 63, Hollandaise, page 66, or Nantua, page 70. Smaller cuts of fish and live shellfish should be placed into boiling court-bouillon, then simmered gently for the required time. This procedure ensures that the cut surfaces of the fish are sealed quickly which prevents the fish losing its juices.

MAKES APPROXIMATELY 1 LITRE (1¾ PINTS)

Marinade Crue pour Viandes de Boucherie ou Venaison

100 g (4 oz) carrot, peeled and sliced
100 g (4 oz) onion, peeled and sliced
40 g (1½ oz) shallot, peeled and sliced
25 g (1 oz) celery, sliced
2 cloves garlic
25 g (1 oz) parsley stalks
1 sprig thyme
½ bay leaf
6 peppercorns
2 cloves
1.25 litres (2¼ pints) white wine
500 ml (18 fl oz) white wine vinegar
250 ml (9 fl oz) oil

*P*lace half of the prepared vegetables in the bottom of a 2.5 litre (4½ pint) receptacle. Season the meat to be marinated and lay on top of the vegetables. Add the remaining ingredients, making sure that the liquid just covers the meat. Keep in a cool place, turning the meat frequently.

Uses

This marinade not only adds flavour to meat but also helps to tenderize it. Joints of meat, particularly beef, which are to be braised benefit from marinating. Saddle and haunch of venison are usually marinated for between 12 hours and 3 days. They should then be wiped dry and spit-roasted.

Variation

A cooked marinade can be made in nearly the same way. Lightly fry the vegetables and herbs in oil until starting to colour. Add 1.5 litres (2½ pints) of white wine and 300 ml (½ pint) white wine vinegar and simmer for 30 minutes. Cool before use.

MAKES APPROXIMATELY 2 LITRES (3½ PINTS)

Les Jus de Rôtis

Gravies to accompany roast meat should be made by deglazing the roasting pan with a little water. This will, however, only yield a small amount of gravy. For a greater quantity, prepare some stock in advance. Place bones and trimmings of the meat to be roasted in a baking tray with a little fat, and roast them until brown. Place the bones and trimmings in a pan; deglaze the tray with a little water and add to the pan. Cover with lukewarm, lightly salted water and bring to the boil. Skim and allow to simmer for 2–4 hours according to the type of bones used, then strain.

Roast the meat in a pan just large enough to hold it to prevent the juices and fat burning. Remove the roast and pour off most, but not all, of the fat. Pour on the required amount of stock and stir well to incorporate all the sediment. Reduce by half, pass through a fine strainer and skim off excess fat. (Some fat should be left in the gravy as this will improve the flavour.)

To make gravy for roast game birds, deglaze the pan with water and a little brandy: this will give just the right game flavour. Alternatively, use Fonds Brun de Veau, page 11, or the method outlined above.

FOUNDATION SAUCES

Sauces Mères or Grandes Sauces de Base

*T*he sauces in this chapter are all sauces in their own right, but they also provide perfect bases for many compound brown and white sauces, and as such play a vital role in classical French cookery. A thorough mastery of the following seven sauces will prove invaluable both for everyday cooking, where something simple but classic is required, and for more specialized dinner party cooking, where compound sauces are often needed.

To achieve excellent results never rush any stage in the process. Cook roux slowly until they are the correct colour; fry diced meat and vegetables carefully so that they brown evenly; allow sauces to simmer very gently to extract the maximum flavour from the ingredients.

Jus de Veau Lié

4 litres (7 pints) Fonds Brun de Veau, page 11
25 g (1 oz) arrowroot

R eserve 100 ml (3½ fl oz) of the cold stock for use later. Bring the rest of the stock to the boil, then allow it to reduce to a quarter of its original volume, leaving approximately 1 litre (1¾ pints).

Dilute the arrowroot in the reserved cold stock, stir into the boiling stock and allow to cook gently for 1 minute. Pass through a fine strainer. The resultant gravy should be transparent and light brown in colour, and have a fresh, clean taste.

Uses
This is an excellent, delicate, all-purpose gravy which complements grilled steaks, lamb and veal cutlets and sweetbreads. A sauce-boat of Jus de Veau Lié can accompany roast and pot-roasted meats, but smaller items such as tournedos usually have just a *cordon* of sauce served with them.

Variations
For small cuts of white meat, ***Jus Lié à l'Estragon*** is often suitable. Infuse 50 g (2 oz) fresh tarragon in 1 litre (1¾ pints) Fonds Brun de Veau, page 11. Pass through a fine strainer and thicken as described above.

The original gravy may also be flavoured with Madeira. This is usually done by using the wine to deglaze a pan used for shallow frying of items of meat and poultry, before adding the Jus de Veau Lié. For Jus Lié Tomaté see the 'Uses' section of Essence de Tomate, page 19. These variations may be finished with butter before serving.

MAKES APPROXIMATELY 1 LITRE (1¾ PINTS)

Sauce Espagnole

50 g (2 oz) clarified butter, page 14
65 g (2½ oz) flour, sifted
2.5 litres (4½ pints) Fonds Brun, page 9
25 g (1 oz) streaky bacon, rinded and chopped
50 g (2 oz) carrot, peeled and roughly chopped
25 g (1 oz) onion, peeled and roughly chopped
1 sprig thyme
1 small bay leaf
50 ml (2 fl oz) dry white wine
100 g (4 oz) tomato purée or 200 g (7 oz) fresh tomatoes,
roughly chopped

Start making this sauce at least one day before you need it. Use the clarified butter and flour to make a Roux Brun, page 14, and allow to cool. Place 1.5 litres (2½ pints) of the Fonds Brun in a heavy pan and bring to the boil. Add the roux, mix well with a wooden spoon or whisk, and bring to the boil, stirring continuously. Turn down the heat and allow the sauce to simmer gently.

Meanwhile, place the bacon in a dry pan and fry to extract the fat. Add the vegetables and herbs and fry until golden brown. Carefully drain off the fat and add these ingredients to the sauce. Deglaze the pan with the white wine, reduce by half and add to the sauce. Allow to simmer gently for 1 hour. Pass the sauce through a conical strainer into another pan, pressing lightly. Add a further 500 ml (18 fl oz) of the Fonds Brun, bring back to the boil and allow to simmer gently for a further 2 hours. Then strain and stir occasionally until cold.

The following day, add the remaining Fonds Brun and the tomato purée or fresh tomatoes. Bring the sauce to the boil, stirring continuously with a wooden spoon or whisk. Allow to simmer gently for 1 hour, skimming carefully. Pass through a fine strainer and stir occasionally until the sauce is quite cold.

MAKES APPROXIMATELY 1 LITRE (1¾ PINTS)

Sauce Demi-glace

600 ml (1 pint) Sauce Espagnole, opposite
300 ml ($\frac{1}{2}$ pint) Fonds Brun, page 9
50 ml (2 fl oz) Glace de Viande, page 16
1 tablespoon sherry, port or Madeira (optional)

*T*his sauce is made by bringing Sauce Espagnole to a final stage of perfection. Heat the Sauce Espagnole; when hot, pour in half the cold Fonds Brun and stir. Particles of fat will solidify and rise to the top. Skim carefully, then repeat the process. Continue to simmer and skim until the sauce has reduced to 400 ml (14 fl oz). Finish with the Glace de Viande and a little fortified wine, if desired.

Uses

This is an extremely useful sauce, to accompany egg dishes, poultry and red meats as well as to provide the foundation for many brown sauces. For the **Sauce Demi-glace Tomatée** required for some recipes either increase the proportion of tomato purée or tomatoes used in the Sauce Espagnole, or add 1 tablespoon tomato purée with the Fonds Brun before making the final reduction.

MAKES APPROXIMATELY 600 ML (1 PINT)

Sauce Velouté

50 g (2 oz) clarified butter, page 14
65 g (2½ oz) flour, sifted
1 litre (1¾ pints) Fonds Blanc, page 10

*U*se the butter and flour to make a Roux Blond, page 14, and allow to cool. Heat the stock and gradually stir into the roux, making sure that you obtain a smooth consistency. Bring to the boil, stirring continuously, and allow to simmer very gently for 1 hour, skimming carefully from time to time. Pass through a fine strainer and, if not required immediately, coat the surface with butter to prevent a skin forming.

Uses

This is an important sauce, providing the foundation for several white sauces including Sauces Suprême, page 29, and Chivry, page 61. It can also be served on its own as a coating sauce for *emincés* of poultry and poached or soft-boiled eggs, or as an accompaniment for delicate items such as sweetbreads. Reduced, the sauce may be used for binding main ingredients in vol-au-vent, tartlets and pies.

Variations

The principal ingredient, the stock, can be replaced with Fonds Blanc de Volaille, page 10, to make *Sauce Velouté de Volaille*, or Fumet de Poisson, page 13, making *Sauce Velouté de Poisson*. When making the latter it should be cooked for 20 minutes only. Sauce Velouté may be finished with various compound butters according to the accompanying dish. For example, when used to bind prawns as a filling for tartlets, finish the sauce with a little Beurre de Crevettes, page 103.
MAKES APPROXIMATELY 900 ML (1½ PINTS)

Sauce Suprême

350 ml (12 fl oz) Sauce Velouté, made with Fonds Blanc de
Volaille, opposite
350 ml (12 fl oz) Fonds Blanc de Volaille, page 10
40 ml (1½ fl oz) Cuisson de Champignons, page 17
120 ml (4 fl oz) double cream
20 g (¾ oz) butter

*P*lace the Sauce Velouté, Fonds Blanc de Volaille and Cuisson de Champignons in a heavy pan. Bring to the boil and reduce quickly, while simultaneously adding two-thirds of the cream, a little at a time, and stirring continuously with a straight-edged wooden spatula. When the sauce has been reduced by one-third, pass it through a fine strainer. Finish the sauce with the remaining cream and the butter.

Uses

This rich, white sauce principally accompanies poached, braised and sautéed poultry, where it may be used either as a coating sauce or served separately. Sauce Suprême is also very acceptable served with lightly seasoned, shallow fried veal cutlets and certain egg dishes. Dishes designated '*à la Reine*' also usually require this sauce. An **Omelette à la Reine** is a classic plain omelette stuffed with cooked, diced chicken, mixed with a little Sauce Suprême. A *cordon* of the sauce is then poured around the omelette before serving

Variation

For an equally delicate, ivory-tinted sauce, add 1½ tablespoons of melted light Glace de Viande, page 16, to the above sauce to give **Sauce Ivoire**. This can be used to coat or accompany poached or braised chicken.

MAKES APPROXIMATELY 500 ML (18 FL OZ)

Sauce Béchamel

65 g (2½ oz) clarified butter, page 14
65 g (2½ oz) flour, sifted
1 litre (1¾ pints) boiling milk
1 onion, peeled and finely sliced
1 sprig thyme
salt
pepper
1 pinch grated nutmeg

Use 50 g (2 oz) of the butter and all the flour to make a Roux Blanc, page 14, and allow to cool. Gradually stir the milk into the roux so as to obtain a smooth consistency and bring to boiling point. Fry the onion gently in the remaining butter but do not allow to brown, then add the thyme, salt, pepper and nutmeg. Add this mixture to the sauce and simmer very gently for 1 hour. Pass through a fine strainer. If you are not going to use the sauce immediately, coat the surface with a little butter to prevent a skin forming.

Uses

Sauce Béchamel provides the foundation for many important compound white sauces such as Sauce à la Crème, page 62, and Sauce Mornay, page 68. On its own, Sauce Béchamel can be served with egg and fish dishes, and its consistency can be adjusted by further reduction or the addition of extra hot milk to make it suitable as a binding, coating or accompanying sauce.

Variation

If the sauce is to be served with meat dishes, particularly chicken and veal, take 65 g (2½ oz) lean, diced veal and stew gently in the butter before adding the onion and flavourings.

MAKES APPROXIMATELY 900 ML (1½ PINTS)

Sauce Tomate

15 g (½ oz) butter
25 g (1 oz) streaky bacon, rinded, diced and blanched
25 g (1 oz) onion, peeled and roughly diced
40 g (1½ oz) carrot, peeled and roughly diced
1 bay leaf
1 sprig thyme
25 g (1 oz) flour
1.5 kg (3 lb 6 oz) ripe tomatoes, squashed
400 ml (14 fl oz) Fonds Blanc, page 10
1 clove garlic, peeled and crushed
1 pinch caster sugar

*M*elt the butter in a flameproof casserole, then add the
bacon and fry gently. Add the vegetables and herbs and fry
until golden brown. Sprinkle with the flour and stir. Cook until
golden brown and allow to cool. Add the rest of the
ingredients, season, then bring to the boil, stirring continuously. Cover with a lid and place in a moderate oven (170°C,
325°F, Gas Mark 3) for 1½–2 hours. Strain into a clean pan, stir
and bring to the boil for a few minutes. If not for immediate use,
coat the surface with butter in order to prevent a skin forming.

MAKES APPROXIMATELY 1 LITRE (1¾ PINTS)

BROWN SAUCES

Sauces Composées, Sauces Brunes

*H*ere are sauces rich in colour and flavour to complement meat, game, fish and duck. Many brown sauces are based on Sauce Demi-glace, but tomato and red wine foundations are also much used.

A sauce should possess excellent texture and consistency as well as flavour. It may seem odd that great care is spent skimming fat from the surface of sauces only to find that butter is incorporated to finish. Butter or compound butters are used to lighten sauces, enrich them and give them a brilliant gloss. Unlike the removed fat, butter is easily suspended in the sauce and should not rise to the surface. Compound butters, of course, add or reinforce a specific flavour as well as having these other properties.

Sauce Bordelaise

300 ml (½ pint) red wine
25 g (1 oz) shallot, peeled and finely chopped
½ bay leaf
1 sprig thyme
coarsely ground black pepper
500 ml (18 fl oz) Sauce Espagnole, page 26
50 g (2 oz) bone marrow, diced
85 ml (3 fl oz) Fonds Blanc, page 10
1 tablespoon melted Glace de Viande, page 16
1 tablespoon lemon juice

*P*lace the wine, shallot, bay leaf and thyme in a small pan, season with black pepper and reduce by three-quarters. Add the Sauce Espagnole and simmer gently for 15 minutes, skimming as necessary.

Poach the bone marrow in the stock, drain and reserve. Pass the sauce through a fine strainer and finish with the melted Glace de Viande, lemon juice and poached marrow.

Uses

Serve Sauce Bordelaise with grilled red meat. For **Tournedos à la Bordelaise**, season and grill the tournedos then arrange them on a dish with a slice of poached bone marrow on top. Sprinkle with parsley and serve with the above sauce.

Variation

For grilled white meat and fish, **Sauce Bordelaise au Vin Blanc** (also known as **Sauce Bonnefoy**) is to be preferred. Prepare this in the same way but replace the red wine with white wine – ideally a dry Graves – and substitute Sauce Velouté, page 28, for the Sauce Espagnole. Finish with a little chopped fresh tarragon.

MAKES APPROXIMATELY 600 ML (1 PINT)

Sauce aux Champignons

175 ml (6 fl oz) Cuisson de Champignons, page 17
500 ml (18 fl oz) Sauce Demi-glace, page 27
75 g (3 oz) button mushrooms
50 g (2 oz) butter

*P*lace the Cuisson de Champignons in a pan and reduce by half. Add the Sauce Demi-glace and simmer gently for a few minutes. Pass through a fine strainer and return to the pan.

Cook the mushrooms in 15 g ($\frac{1}{2}$ oz) of the butter. Finish the sauce with the remaining butter to give a glossy sheen and finally add the cooked mushrooms.

Uses

Serve this sauce with small cuts of meat, such as grilled steaks, as well as with sautéed poultry or grilled fish. The larger fillet of beef also takes the sauce well. Flavour Sauce aux Champignons with a dash of Madeira and the cooking juices from a *poêléd* fillet, and serve the fillet garnished with large grooved mushrooms cooked in butter. This dish is known as **Filet de Boeuf au Madère et aux Champignons**.

Variation

A **Sauce Blanche aux Champignons** can be made by replacing the Sauce Demi-glace with 400 ml (14 fl oz) Sauce Allemande, page 53. Reduce the Cuisson de Champignons by two-thirds before adding the Sauce Allemande, then proceed as above. The button mushrooms added to finish should be grooved and cooked, though kept very white. Serve with poultry.

MAKES APPROXIMATELY 600 ML (1 PINT)

Sauce Chasseur

75 g (3 oz) button mushrooms, sliced
15 g ($\frac{1}{2}$ oz) butter
25 ml (1 fl oz) olive oil
15 g ($\frac{1}{2}$ oz) shallot, peeled and finely chopped
100 ml (3$\frac{1}{2}$ fl oz) white wine
25 ml (1 fl oz) brandy
200 ml (7 fl oz) Sauce Demi-glace, page 27
100 ml (3$\frac{1}{2}$ fl oz) Sauce Tomate, page 31
2 teaspoons Glace de Viande, page 16
1 teaspoon chopped fresh parsley

Cook the mushrooms until lightly coloured in the butter and oil. Add the shallot and cook together for a few minutes. Drain off half of the fat and moisten with the wine and brandy. Reduce by half, then stir in the Sauce Demi-glace, Sauce Tomate and Glace de Viande. Simmer gently for 5 minutes, and finish with the chopped parsley.

Uses

This is a marvellous sauce with many applications, from coating soft-boiled eggs to accompanying most sautéed meats. It can be served in a sauceboat or, as in **Poulet Sauté Chasseur**, as part of a sauced dish: joint a chicken, season the pieces and cook quickly in hot oil and butter. Arrange in a *timbale*, cover and keep warm. Using the same pan, prepare a Sauce Chasseur with the addition of a pinch each of chopped tarragon and chervil. Pour over the chicken and sprinkle with chopped parsley.

Variations

This sauce recipe, which was Escoffier's own special creation, can be made without the brandy, and the Glace de Viande can be replaced with extra butter for finishing, although these changes will not improve upon the original.

MAKES APPROXIMATELY 350 ML (12 FL OZ)

Sauce Chateaubriand

450 ml (¾ pint) white wine
20 g (¾ oz) shallot, peeled and chopped
1 pinch chopped fresh thyme
a small piece bay leaf
40 g (1½ oz) mushroom trimmings
450 ml (¾ pint) Fonds Brun de Veau, page 11
120 g (4½ oz) Beurre à la Maître d'Hôtel, page 105
1 teaspoon chopped fresh tarragon

*P*lace the wine in a pan with the shallot, thyme, bay leaf and mushroom trimmings and reduce by two-thirds. Add the Fonds Brun de Veau, bring to the boil and reduce again by half. Pass through a fine strainer, and finish with the Beurre à la Maître d'Hôtel and the chopped tarragon.

Uses

This sauce is served with grilled red meat, particularly grilled tournedos. As a general rule, Sauce Chateaubriand is the correct accompanying sauce if the tournedos are accompanied by a vegetable garnish such as **Subrics d'Epinard** (cooked spinach mixed with Sauce Béchamel, page 30, double cream and egg yolks and seasoned with nutmeg; tablespoons of this mixture are then shallow fried in butter), artichokes or a purée of haricot beans. This sauce is also associated with dishes garnished in the '**Mirette**' manner: small dice of potatoes are cooked in butter then mixed with a *julienne* of truffle and a little melted Glace de Viande, page 16; this mixture is used to fill buttered dariole moulds which are, when demoulded, sprinkled with Parmesan cheese, dotted with butter and quickly gratinated.

In effect, Sauce Chateaubriand is a buttered meat glaze containing chopped fresh parsley and tarragon and should not be confused with Sauce or Beurre Colbert, page 105, which is Beurre à la Maître d'Hôtel with a small addition of meat glaze.

MAKES APPROXIMATELY 300 ML (½ PINT)

Sauce Chaud-froid Brune

400 ml (14 fl oz) Sauce Demi-glace, page 27
50 ml (2 fl oz) Essence de Truffes, page 17
350 ml (12 fl oz) Gelée Ordinaire, clarified, pages 92 and 96
salt
pepper
25 ml (1 fl oz) Madeira or port wine

*P*lace the Demi-glace and Essence de Truffes in a pan and reduce rapidly whilst stirring in the Gelée Ordinaire. Allow the reduction to continue until you are left with approximately 500 ml (18 fl oz) of sauce. Adjust the seasoning with salt and pepper and finish away from the heat with the Madeira or port wine.

Pass through a fine strainer and cool until a coating consistency is reached. Stir the sauce frequently until ready for use.

Uses

This is not used as widely as Sauce Chaud-froid, page 59, but is used for coating various cold meats and hors d'oeuvre such as tiny choux paste éclairs filled with puréed game.

MAKES APPROXIMATELY 500 ML (18 FL OZ)

Sauce Diable

300 ml ($\frac{1}{2}$ pint) white wine
20 g ($\frac{3}{4}$ oz) shallot, peeled and finely chopped
200 ml (7 fl oz) Sauce Demi-glace, page 27
cayenne pepper

*P*lace the wine and shallot in a small pan, bring to the boil and reduce by two thirds. Add the Sauce Demi-glace, season generously with cayenne pepper and simmer for a few minutes. Reserve for use.

Uses

Sauce Diable has many applications. The strong flavour complements grilled chicken and pigeon dishes very well. A good example of this is **Poulet de Grains Grillé Diable**: split a spring chicken along the backbone and open it out. Season, brush with butter and place in the oven until half-cooked. Coat with Dijon mustard, sprinkle with cayenne pepper and coat with breadcrumbs. Spoon melted butter over before finishing under the grill. Serve with slices of lemon and the above sauce. Grilled steaks and hamburgers also benefit from the spicy sauce as an accompaniment. More surprising perhaps is the happy marriage of Sauce Diable with fish, in particular grilled fillets of plaice and sole, and whole red mullet.

Variations

White wine vinegar may be used to replace all or half of the wine in the recipe and 1 tablespoon finely chopped *fines herbes* may be added with the shallot. If all vinegar is used, though, the initial reduction should be taken a stage further until the shallot is almost dry before adding the Demi-glace, or the sauce will taste unpalatably sour.

MAKES APPROXIMATELY 300 ML ($\frac{1}{2}$ PINT)

Sauce Estragon

100 ml (3½ fl oz) white wine
20 g (¾ oz) fresh tarragon leaves
275 ml (9 fl oz) Sauce Demi-glace, page 27
1 teaspoon chopped fresh tarragon

*B*ring the wine to the boil and add the tarragon leaves. Cover the pan, remove from the heat and allow to infuse for 10 minutes. Add the Sauce Demi-glace, bring back to the boil and reduce by one third. Pass through a fine strainer and finish with the chopped tarragon.

Uses

This sauce can be served with small cuts of white meat and egg dishes. It is the perfect partner for sautéed chicken, as in **Poulet Sauté à l'Estragon**: season prepared joints of chicken and sauté them in butter. Place in a deep dish, then deglaze the pan with the infused tarragon wine and proceed to make up the sauce as above, but without the chopped tarragon. Pour this over the chicken and garnish with blanched leaves of tarragon.

Variations

If fresh tarragon leaves are unavailable, dried tarragon may be used in the infusion, although the resultant sauce will not have such a clean taste. For a more delicate sauce, replace the Sauce Demi-glace with Jus de Veau Lié, page 25.

MAKES APPROXIMATELY 275 ML (9 FL OZ)

Sauce aux Fines Herbes

150 ml ($\frac{1}{4}$ pint) white wine
20 g ($\frac{3}{4}$ oz) mixed sprigs fresh parsley, chives, chervil and
tarragon, in equal quantities
300 ml ($\frac{1}{2}$ pint) Sauce Demi-glace, page 27
1 heaped tablespoon mixed and finely chopped fresh parsley,
chives, chervil and tarragon, in equal quantities
squeeze of lemon juice

*P*lace the wine and sprigs of herbs in a small pan and bring to the boil. Cover the pan, remove from the heat and allow to infuse for 20 minutes. Pass through a clean cloth and add to the Sauce Demi-glace. Simmer gently for 5 minutes. Just before serving, finish the sauce with the finely chopped herbs and lemon juice.

Uses

Traditionally this sauce is served with various preparations of veal designated '*aux Fines Herbes*'. For *Foie de Veau* or *Côte de Veau aux Fines Herbes*, season and, where necessary, flour the principal ingredient then shallow fry in butter. Deglaze the pan with a little white wine, then stir in the Sauce aux Fines Herbes, simmer and use to accompany the dish. This sauce is also one of many which is suitable for serving with *emincés*.

Variations

Sauce aux Fines Herbes for Fish: add 40 g ($1\frac{1}{2}$ oz) Beurre d'Echalote, page 102, and 2 teaspoons chopped *fines herbes* to 450 ml ($\frac{3}{4}$ pint) Sauce Vin Blanc, page 79. This makes an excellent accompaniment for white fish, particularly poached fillets of whiting and sole, and paupiettes of sole.

MAKES 450 ML ($\frac{3}{4}$ PINT)

Sauce Grand-Veneur

500 ml (18 fl oz) thin Sauce Poivrade for Game, page 46
135 ml (4½ fl oz) double cream
1 tablespoon redcurrant jelly

*H*eat the Sauce Poivrade. Just before serving, stir the double cream and redcurrant jelly into the sauce. Mix well.

Uses

Serve Sauce Grand-Veneur with roast joints of venison. Use either leg, haunch or saddle of venison and lard carefully with salt pork fat. Marinate for about 12 hours in a suitable marinade, page 22, then roast or spit-roast in a hot oven (220°C, 425°F, Gas Mark 7), basting as necessary. Cook for 15–18 minutes per kg (2 lb), keeping the meat pink and slightly underdone.

Variation

Instead of adding cream and redcurrant jelly, 50 ml (2 fl oz) of hare's blood and 50 ml (2 fl oz) of the marinade may be added to the Sauce Poivrade. This mixture should be heated to cook the blood and thicken the sauce. Strain and use as above.

MAKES APPROXIMATELY 600 ML (1 PINT)

Sauce Gratin

15 g (½ oz) each onion and shallot, peeled and finely chopped
15 g (½ oz) butter
1 tablespoon oil
100 g (4 oz) mushrooms, finely chopped
1 pinch finely chopped fresh parsley
150 ml (¼ pint) white wine
150 ml (¼ pint) Fumet de Poisson, page 13, made with the bones
and trimmings of the fish under preparation
1 tablespoon chopped shallot
275 ml (9 fl oz) Sauce Demi-glace, page 27
2 teaspoons chopped fresh parsley

First cook the onion and shallot in the butter and oil for a few minutes, then add the mushroom trimmings. Cook until dry, season and add the pinch of chopped parsley. Reserve. Combine the wine and Fumet de Poisson and add the shallot. Boil and reduce by half. Add the mushroom mixture and Sauce Demi-glace and simmer for 5–6 minutes. Finish with chopped parsley.

Uses
This sauce is suitable for the preparation of fish '***au Gratin***' using sole, whiting, etc. The fish should be pre-cooked then placed in a buttered dish containing a little Sauce Gratin. Place sliced raw mushrooms on the fish, coat with more sauce then sprinkle with white wine, breadcrumbs and melted butter. Bake in a moderate oven (180°C, 350°F, Gas Mark 4) until the fish has reheated and a golden crust has formed on the top.

Variation
Sauce Duxelles should be used for meat and vegetable dishes designated '***au Gratin***'. Replace the Fumet de Poisson with Cuisson de Champignons, page 17, and add ½ tablespoon tomato purée with the Sauce Demi-glace.

MAKES APPROXIMATELY 450 ML (¾ PINT)

Sauce Hachée

50 g (2 oz) butter
100 g (4 oz) mushrooms, finely chopped
50 g (2 oz) onion, peeled and chopped
25 g (1 oz) shallot, peeled and chopped
100 ml (3½ fl oz) vinegar
200 ml (7 fl oz) Sauce Espagnole, page 26
65 ml (2½ fl oz) Sauce Tomate, page 31
1 tablespoon chopped lean cooked ham
1 tablespoon small capers
1 teaspoon chopped fresh parsley

First heat 25 g (1 oz) of the butter in a small pan, add the mushrooms and cook gently until all the moisture has evaporated. Lightly season and reserve for use later.

Soften the onion and shallot in the remaining butter, then moisten with the vinegar and reduce by half. Add the Sauce Espagnole and Sauce Tomate and simmer for 5 minutes. Finish the sauce with the ham, capers, prepared mushrooms and chopped parsley, and check the seasoning.

Uses
This sauce can be served with grilled, roast or boiled pork. It can also accompany boiled beef and beef, lamb and pork *emincés*.

Variation
Another sauce with similar uses is ***Sauce Piquante***: take 150 ml (¼ pint) white wine, an equal quantity of vinegar and 25 g (1 oz) chopped shallot and reduce by half. Add 600 ml (1 pint) Sauce Espagnole, page 26, bring to the boil and simmer gently for 10 minutes. Skim as necessary and finish with 1 tablespoon mixed chopped gherkins, fresh tarragon, chervil and parsley.

MAKES APPROXIMATELY 350 ML (12 FL OZ)

Sauce Lyonnaise

50 g (2 oz) butter
250 g (9 oz) onion, peeled and evenly chopped
200 ml (7 fl oz) white wine
200 ml (7 fl oz) vinegar
750 ml (1¼ pints) Sauce Demi-glace, page 27

*H*eat the butter in a pan and add the chopped onion. Cook slowly, stirring occasionally, until the onion is golden brown. Moisten with the wine and vinegar, bring to the boil and reduce by two-thirds. Add the Sauce Demi-glace and simmer gently, skimming as necessary, for 5–6 minutes. Pass through a fine strainer and reserve for use.

Uses
Sauce Lyonnaise is normally served with small cuts of red meat and *emincés* of beef. It can also accompany grilled hamburgers.

MAKES APPROXIMATELY 750 ML (1¼ PINTS)

Sauce Madère

500 ml (18 fl oz) Sauce Demi-glace, page 27
50 ml (2 fl oz) dry Madeira

Reduce the Sauce Demi-glace by approximately one-tenth of its volume, or until it has thickened slightly. Remove from the heat and add the Madeira. Pass through a fine strainer and do not reboil before use.

Uses
This is a particularly useful sauce that can be served with a wide variety of meats. Those that benefit especially from Sauce Madère are roasted fillet of beef, braised ox tongue and braised chicken. For extra flavour, the braising or cooking liquor from the meat can be reduced, strained and added to the sauce. Although not usually required, the sauce may be finished with butter to give it a glossier appearance.

Variations
To make **Sauce Financière**, reduce 500 ml (18 fl oz) Sauce Madère by a quarter, remove from the heat and add 40 ml (1½ fl oz) Essence de Truffes, page 17, then pass through a fine strainer. This sauce is normally associated with dishes garnished '*à la Financière*' (with veal or chicken quenelles, small grooved mushrooms, mixed cockscombs and kidneys, slices of truffle and blanched olives). With or without the garnish the sauce is suitable for serving with braised loin or cushion of veal, cuts or joints of meat and poultry and braised sweetbreads.

Sauce au Porto is prepared as for Sauce Madère, replacing the Madeira with port. Serve with any of the dishes mentioned above for Sauce Madère, as well as with wild duck, goose and pheasant.

MAKES APPROXIMATELY 500 ML (18 FL OZ)

Sauce Poivrade

25 ml (1 fl oz) oil
175 g (6 oz) mirepoix, comprising 90 g (3½ oz) carrot, peeled
and diced; 50 g (2 oz) onion, peeled and diced; a few parsley
stalks; 1 small pinch chopped fresh thyme; and
½ bay leaf, crushed
50 ml (2 fl oz) wine vinegar
200 ml (7 fl oz) dry white wine
500 ml (18 fl oz) Sauce Espagnole, page 26
6 peppercorns, crushed
25 g (1 oz) butter

*H*eat the oil in a pan, add the *mirepoix* of vegetables and herbs and fry until lightly coloured. Add the wine vinegar and half of the wine and reduce by two-thirds. Add the Sauce Espagnole and simmer gently for 10 minutes, then add the peppercorns and cook for a further 10 minutes. Pass through a strainer, pressing firmly, then add the rest of the wine. Bring to the boil, skim and simmer gently for a further 10 minutes or so until reduced to about 450 ml (¾ pint). Pass through a fine strainer again, finish with the butter and check seasoning.

Uses
This sauce is ideal for serving with joints of roast beef or venison, whether marinated or not. If marinated, the marinating liquid should be used instead of the wine.

Variation
To make **Sauce Poivrade for Game**, fry 225 g (8 oz) of venison trimmings with the *mirepoix*, use equal quantities of wine vinegar and dry white wine, and finally use half Fonds de Gibier, page 12, one quarter Sauce Espagnole and one quarter marinade from the game joint in preparation instead of Sauce Espagnole alone, as in the recipe above.

MAKES APPROXIMATELY 450 ML (¾ PINT)

Sauce Provençale

100 ml (3½ fl oz) olive oil
800 g (1¾ lb) tomatoes, peeled, depipped and roughly chopped
1 pinch caster sugar
1 clove garlic, peeled and crushed
1 tablespoon chopped fresh parsley

*H*eat the oil in a pan until almost smoking hot. Add the chopped tomato flesh and season. Add the sugar, garlic and parsley. Cover with a lid and simmer gently for 30 minutes.

Uses
This is used as the accompanying sauce for dishes garnished '*à la Provençale*', together with 10 small tomatoes and 10 large mushrooms, stuffed with a chopped mushroom mixture containing a little garlic. Veal cutlets, shallow fried tournedos and poultry can all be served with this garnish and sauce. Another garnish that includes Sauce Provençale is '*à la Marseillaise*'; also included in this garnish are halved, hollowed tomatoes cooked with a little garlic and containing a stuffed olive and fillet of anchovy each and copeaux potatoes (deep-fried potato ribbons).

Variations
Sauce Provençale can also accompany fish, in which case some of the reduced fish poaching liquor is usually added, as in *Sole à la Provençale*. Prepare and shallow poach the fish in a buttered dish with 100 ml (3½ fl oz) Fumet de Poisson, page 13, 2 tablespoons olive oil and a touch of crushed garlic. When cooked, drain and place the sole in a dish surrounded with stuffed tomatoes. Reduce the cooking liquor by two-thirds and add to 275 ml (9 fl oz) of Sauce Provençale. Use this to coat the fish, then sprinkle with finely chopped parsley.

MAKES APPROXIMATELY 500 ML (18 FL OZ)

Sauce Robert

40 g (1½ oz) butter
150 g (5 oz) onion, peeled and finely chopped
200 ml (7 fl oz) dry white wine
300 ml (½ pint) Sauce Demi-glace, page 27
1 pinch sugar
1 teaspoon dry English mustard, diluted with a little water

*H*eat the butter in a pan and cook the onion until soft but not coloured. Moisten with the wine and reduce by two-thirds. Add the Sauce Demi-glace and simmer gently for 10 minutes. Pass through a fine strainer and finish away from the heat with the sugar and mustard. Do not re-boil the sauce once the mustard has been added.

Uses

Serve Sauce Robert with pork, especially grilled pork cutlets.

Variations

To the above sauce add 50 g (2 oz) gherkins, cut into a thick, short *julienne*, just before serving. This variation is called **Sauce Charcutière** and can also accompany pork, as in **Côtes de Porc Charcutière**: flatten some pork cutlets, season, dip in melted butter and breadcrumbs then grill them gently. Arrange around a dish and place a mound of mashed potato in the centre. Accompany with Sauce Charcutière.

In both of these sauces it is not strictly necessary to strain out the chopped onion. Whether this is done or not is a matter of personal preference.

MAKES APPROXIMATELY 450 ML (¾ PINT)

Sauce Romaine

50 g (2 oz) sugar
150 ml ($\frac{1}{4}$ pint) vinegar
600 ml (1 pint) Sauce Espagnole, page 26
300 ml ($\frac{1}{2}$ pint) Fonds de Gibier, page 12
20 g ($\frac{3}{4}$ oz) sultanas
20 g ($\frac{3}{4}$ oz) currants
20 g ($\frac{3}{4}$ oz) pine nuts, toasted

Place the sugar in a pan and cook gently to a golden caramel colour. Immediately add the vinegar and continue to cook, stirring, until the sugar has dissolved. Mix in the Sauce Espagnole and Fonds de Gibier and reduce by one-third. Soak the dried fruit in warm water until plump, then drain. Strain the sauce and finish with the toasted pine nuts and fruit.

Uses

This sauce is usually served with joints of venison. It may also be adapted for use with roast, marinated joints of beef and mutton by replacing the Fonds de Gibier with Fonds Brun, page 9.

MAKES APPROXIMATELY 600 ML (1 PINT)

Sauce au Vin Rouge

65 g (2½ oz) vegetable, herb and bacon mirepoix
75 g (3 oz) butter
275 ml (9 fl oz) good red wine
½ clove garlic, peeled and crushed
400 ml (14 fl oz) Sauce Espagnole, page 26
½ teaspoon anchovy essence
cayenne pepper

Lightly stew the *mirepoix* in 25 g (1 oz) butter, then moisten with the wine. Reduce by half. Add the garlic and stir in the Sauce Espagnole. Skim carefully and simmer gently for 10 minutes. Pass through a fine strainer and finish with the remaining butter and the anchovy essence. Season with a touch of cayenne pepper.

Uses
This is a true red wine sauce and is particularly suited to poached fish dishes. It may, however, also accompany meat, poultry and egg dishes.

Variations
Sauce Bourguignonne is another red wine sauce, and one that can be especially suitable for serving with poached and soft-boiled eggs. Place 900 ml (1½ pints) red wine in a pan with 40 g (1½ oz) sliced shallot, thyme, parsley stalks and 15 g (½ oz) mushroom trimmings. Reduce by half and strain into a clean pan. Thicken with *beurre manié* made with 25 g (1 oz) butter and 20 g (¾ oz) flour. Finish at the last minute with 75 g (3 oz) butter and a touch of cayenne pepper.

MAKES APPROXIMATELY 500 ML (18 FL OZ)

Sauce Zingara

135 ml (4½ fl oz) vinegar
1 scant tablespoon finely chopped shallot
350 ml (12 fl oz) Fonds Brun, page 9
75 g (3 oz) fresh breadcrumbs
40 g (1½ oz) butter
½ tablespoon chopped fresh parsley
1 tablespoon lemon juice

*P*lace the vinegar in a small pan with the shallot and reduce by half. Moisten with the Fonds Brun and simmer gently. Meanwhile, fry the breadcrumbs in the butter until golden, then add to the sauce. Finish with the chopped parsley and lemon juice.

Uses
Serve this sauce with entrées of veal and poultry.

Variations
Another sauce with the same name and similar uses is made as follows: reduce 65 ml (2½ fl oz) each white wine and Cuisson de Champignons, page 17, by two-thirds. Add 200 ml (7 fl oz) Sauce Demi-glace, page 27, 120 ml (4 fl oz) Sauce Tomate, page 31, and 50 ml (2 fl oz) Fonds Blanc, page 10. Simmer for 5 minutes, skim carefully and season with a little cayenne pepper. Finish the sauce with a *julienne* comprising 40 g (1½ oz) cooked ham and salted ox tongue, 25 g (1 oz) mushrooms and 15 g (½ oz) truffle. This mixed *julienne* forms the '***Zingara***' garnish, and is usually served with veal accompanied by Sauce Demi-glace, page 27, flavoured with tomato and tarragon.

MAKES APPROXIMATELY 450 ML (¾ PINT)

WHITE
SAUCES

Sauces Composées, Sauces Blanches

*T*he sauces in this chapter are generally light and are suitable for serving with poultry, veal, fish, eggs and vegetables. Consequently they tend to be based on light stocks, white wine and dairy products. There are exceptions, of course, such as Sauce Smitane, page 74, which makes a perfect accompaniment for sautéed game.

Herbs play an important role in many white sauces both as a flavouring and colouring ingredient. Use fresh herbs whenever possible.

If sauces are not required immediately they can be kept warm in a *bain-marie*, stirring occasionally to prevent a skin forming, or covering the surface with a disc of greaseproof paper.

Sauce Allemande

275 ml (9 fl oz) Fonds Blanc, page 10
100 ml (3½ fl oz) Cuisson de Champignons, page 17
3 small egg yolks
a squeeze of lemon juice
1 pinch coarsely ground black pepper
1 pinch grated nutmeg
500 ml (18 fl oz) Sauce Velouté, page 28
50 g (2 oz) butter

*P*lace the Fonds Blanc, Cuisson de Champignons, egg yolks and flavourings in a heavy shallow pan. Mix well with a whisk, then add the Sauce Velouté. Bring to the boil, stirring continuously, then reduce the heat and cook until the sauce has reduced by one-third or until it is thick enough just to coat the back of the spoon. Pass through a fine strainer. Whisk in the butter, cut into small pieces, and use the sauce as required.

If you are not going to use the sauce immediately, coat the surface with 15 g (½ oz) of the butter to prevent a skin forming. Keep the sauce warm in a *bain-marie*, and whisk in the remaining butter, cut into small pieces, just before serving.

Uses

The subtle flavour of this sauce complements delicate items like sweetbreads, poached chicken, eggs and vegetables very well. Sauce Allemande may also be used as a binding sauce in hot pies and vol-au-vent. For **Croûtes aux Champignons**, mix the sauce with button mushrooms which have been lightly cooked in butter and lemon juice, and use this mixture to fill croûtes (thick slices of bread partially hollowed out, spread with butter and cooked until crisp in the oven).

MAKES APPROXIMATELY 600 ML (1 PINT)

Sauce Aurore

400 ml (14 fl oz) Sauce Velouté, page 28
150 ml (¼ pint) fresh tomato purée
50 g (2 oz) butter

*W*arm the Sauce Velouté and add the tomato purée. Bring to the boil and simmer for a few minutes, finishing away from the heat with the butter.

Uses

This tasty, pink sauce can be served with poached chicken, sweetbreads and egg dishes. There are several ways of preparing **Oeufs à l'Aurore**: for soft-boiled or poached eggs, coat the eggs with the sauce and set on round or oval puff pastry bases. For hard-boiled eggs, cut the eggs in half lengthwise and remove the yolks. Pound these with an equal quantity of cold Sauce Béchamel, page 30, and butter, and season with salt, pepper and chopped *fines herbes*. Fill the egg whites with this mixture and place on a dish coated with Sauce Mornay, page 68; sprinkle with grated cheese and melted butter and gratinate. Surround with a *cordon* of Sauce Aurore.

MAKES APPROXIMATELY 600 ML (1 PINT)

Sauce Béarnaise

100 ml (3½ fl oz) dry white wine
100 ml (3½ fl oz) tarragon vinegar
2 tablespoons chopped shallot
6 peppercorns, crushed
2 tablespoons chopped fresh tarragon
1 tablespoon chopped fresh chervil
4 egg yolks
300 g (11 oz) butter, softened
salt
cayenne pepper

Place the wine and the vinegar in a small pan with the shallot, peppercorns and half the herbs. Bring to the boil and reduce to a quarter of its original volume. Allow to cool.

Whisk the egg yolks into the reduction and, over a gentle heat, gradually whisk in the butter. When all the butter has been incorporated and the sauce is very thick, pass through a fine strainer, correct the seasoning and add a little cayenne pepper. Finish by stirring in the remaining herbs. Do not allow the sauce to reach a temperature much higher than blood heat, or it will curdle. If the sauce does become too hot and separates, it may be reconstituted by whisking in a few drops of cold water. If not required immediately, keep the sauce warm in a *bain-marie*, whisking occasionally. Serve lukewarm.

Uses
Typically, Sauce Béarnaise is served with grilled steaks and lamb cutlets, giving an excellent combination of flavours.

Variation
When flavoured with up to 65 ml (2½ fl oz) of fresh tomato purée, Sauce Béarnaise becomes **Sauce Choron** or **Sauce Béarnaise Tomatée**. Serve this with grilled steaks and poultry.

MAKES APPROXIMATELY 300 ML (½ PINT)

Sauce Bercy

1 tablespoon finely chopped shallot
75 g (3 oz) butter
135 ml (4½ fl oz) white wine
135 ml (4½ fl oz) Fumet de Poisson, page 13
350 ml (12 fl oz) Sauce Velouté de Poisson, page 28
½ tablespoon chopped fresh parsley

Stew the shallot in 25 g (1 oz) butter until soft but not coloured. Moisten with the white wine and Fumet de Poisson and reduce by one-third. Stir in the Velouté de Poisson and bring to the boil. Simmer for 5 minutes, then remove from the heat and finish with the remaining butter and parsley.

Uses
Serve this sauce with whole or large pieces of baked cod, shad or perch. For serving with poached fish, replace the Fumet de Poisson with an equal quantity of poaching liquor.

Variations
Sauce Marinière is a fish sauce based on Sauce Bercy and suitable for serving with fish and shellfish and as a sauce in hot tartlets and vol-au-vent. To make, add 50 ml (2 fl oz) reduced mussel cooking liquor to the above sauce, then thicken using 3 egg yolks as a liaison. Whisk briskly over a gentle heat taking care that the sauce does not boil. For the classic **Moules à la Marinière**, cook the mussels in the usual manner, then remove one of the shells from each mussel. Prepare Sauce Marinière but omit the liaison. Stir the mussels into the sauce and sharpen with a few drops of lemon juice. Place in a deep dish and serve sprinkled with parsley.

MAKES APPROXIMATELY 500 ML (18 FL OZ)

Sauce au Beurre

175 g (6 oz) butter
20 g (¾ oz) flour, sifted
350 ml (12 fl oz) boiling water
1 pinch salt
2 large egg yolks
25 ml (1 fl oz) double cream
squeeze lemon juice

Melt 20 g (¾ oz) butter in a pan and stir in the flour. Add the boiling water gradually, whisking thoroughly after each addition, and season. Make a liaison using the egg yolks, cream and lemon juice, and add this to the sauce. Reheat gently until the mixture thickens, stirring continuously and taking care not to let it boil. Pass through a fine strainer and finish with the remaining butter. If not for immediate use, keep the sauce warm in a *bain-marie*, only adding the butter at the last moment.

Uses

This sauce, also known as **Sauce Batârde**, is served with boiled vegetables, particularly asparagus, and delicately flavoured poached fish such as John Dory, plaice and sole.

MAKES APPROXIMATELY 500 ML (18 FL OZ)

Sauce Canotière

900 ml (1½ pints) reserved Court-bouillon au Vin Blanc,
page 20, used for poaching fish
50 g (2 oz) butter
10 g (¼ oz) flour
cayenne pepper

*P*lace the reserved court-bouillon in a pan and reduce by two-thirds. Prepare a *beurre manié* using 15 g (½ oz) soft butter and the flour. Whisk this into the boiling reduction a little at a time, and stir until it thickens. Remove from the heat, pass through a fine strainer and finish the sauce with the rest of the butter and a small pinch of cayenne pepper. Adjust the seasoning with a pinch of salt if necessary.

Uses

Sauce Canotière is usually served with poached or boiled freshwater fish and also provides the final sauce for a matelote (a type of fish stew). For **Matelote à la Canotière**, take 750 g (1½ lb) pieces of cleaned carp and eel and place in pan with a few slices of onion, a bouquet garni, 1 clove garlic, salt and 2 peppercorns. Moisten with 500 ml (18 fl oz) white wine and flame with 25 ml (1 fl oz) brandy. Cover the pan and cook gently until the fish is cooked. Lift the fish into a serving dish and keep warm. Strain the cooking liquor and use to make Sauce Canotière as above. Pour over the fish and garnish with mushrooms, glazed button onions, crispy deep-fried gudgeon and poached crayfish.

Variation

With the addition of small glazed onions and button mushrooms, Sauce Canotière can be used as a simpler version of **Sauce Matelote Blanche**, page 20.

MAKES APPROXIMATELY 300 ML (½ PINT)

Sauce Chaud-froid

400 ml (14 fl oz) Sauce Velouté, page 28
300–350 ml (10–12 fl oz) Gelée de Volaille, clarified,
pages 93 and 97
150 ml (¼ pint) double cream
salt
pepper

*P*lace the Sauce Velouté in a shallow pan and reduce rapidly whilst stirring continuously. Gradually stir in the Gelée de Volaille with 50 ml (2 fl oz) of the cream. Reduce over a moderate heat by approximately one-third, correct the seasoning and strain. Finish with the remaining cream and stir continuously until cold and of a coating consistency.

Uses

This sauce is used to coat special cold dishes, usually poultry, joints of ham and egg dishes. Once the correct consistency has been reached it is important to apply the sauce quickly and carefully, before it begins to set. To prolong this period, place the container of sauce in a bowl of tepid water. Items coated with the sauce may then be decorated with blanched leaves of tarragon, thin slices of mushroom, grooved carrot, or similar items and finally coated with a thin layer of Gelée de Volaille.

Variations

For coating whole cold fish or cutlets of cold fish, **Sauce Chaud-froid for Fish** should be used. Follow the recipe above but replace the Sauce Velouté with Sauce Velouté de Poisson, page 28, and use Gelée de Poisson, page 95, instead of the Gelée de Volaille. Other variations for Sauce Chaud-froid are given beneath Sauce Chaud-froid Blonde, page 60.

MAKES APPROXIMATELY 500 ML (18 FL OZ)

Sauce Chaud-froid Blonde

400 ml (14 fl oz) Sauce Allemande, page 53
300–350 ml (10–12 fl oz) Gelée de Volaille, clarified,
pages 93 and 97
100 ml (3½ fl oz) double cream
salt
pepper

*P*lace the Sauce Allemande in a shallow pan and reduce rapidly. Gradually stir in the Gelée de Volaille with half of the cream. Reduce over a moderate heat by one-third, correct the seasoning and strain. Finish with the remaining cream and stir continuously until cool and of a coating consistency.

Uses
This sauce can be used to coat cold items of food such as poultry, ham and egg dishes. The remarks concerning the use of Sauce Chaud-froid on page 59 are also applicable to this sauce.

Variations
For a **Sauce Chaud-froid Aurore**, prepare Sauce Chaud-froid, page 59, with the addition of 65 ml (2½ fl oz) of very red fresh tomato purée, passed through muslin, and a pinch of paprika infused in 1 tablespoon stock. Add these to the reduction and cook until you are left with about 500 ml (18 fl oz) of sauce. This sauce is used to coat special preparations of cold poultry.

Dishes designated '**Chauds-froids Printaniers**' usually use **Sauce Chaud-froid au Vert-pré**: make an infusion with 85 ml (3 fl oz) white wine and a good pinch of *fines herbes* and strain through muslin. Add this slowly to the reduction in Sauce Chaud-froid, page 59, with the Gelée de Volaille and reduce to 500 ml (18 fl oz). Finish the sauce with a little natural green colour prepared from spinach (see Beurre Colorant Vert, page 102) so as to give a pale green colour to the sauce.

MAKES APPROXIMATELY 500 ML (18 FL OZ)

Sauce Chivry

50 ml (2 fl oz) white wine
1 small pinch each fresh chervil, tarragon, parsley, chives
and young salad burnet
1 teaspoon finely chopped shallot
450 ml (¾ pint) Sauce Velouté, page 28
25 g (1 oz) Beurre Chivry, page 101

Place the wine in a pan and bring to the boil, then add the herbs and finely chopped shallot. Remove from the heat and allow to infuse for 10 minutes. Squeeze the infusion through a clean cloth and reserve. Bring the Sauce Velouté to the boil and stir in the infusion. Finish, off the heat, with the Beurre Chivry.

Uses

Serve Sauce Chivry with poached or boiled poultry, or eggs. For **Oeufs Chivry**, make a purée from cooked spinach, watercress and sorrel mixed with a little Sauce Béchamel, page 30. Reheat with butter and place a little in cooked tartlet cases. Top each case with a soft-boiled or poached egg and coat with Sauce Chivry.

MAKES APPROXIMATELY 500 ML (18 FL OZ)

Sauce à la Crème

600 ml (1 pint) Sauce Béchamel, page 30
250 ml (8 fl oz) double cream
½ tablespoon fresh lemon juice
salt
pepper

*P*lace the Sauce Béchamel in a pan with 150 ml (¼ pint) of the cream. Bring to the boil and reduce to 500 ml (18 fl oz), stirring continuously. Pass through a fine strainer and adjust the consistency by gradually stirring in the remaining cream and lemon juice. Check the seasoning.

Uses

This sauce is suitable for serving with boiled and poached fish, poultry, vegetables and eggs. To finish vegetables with Sauce à la Crème, first drain the vegetables (which should only be lightly cooked) and return them to the pan with enough boiling double cream to coat them well. Cook until the vegetables are tender and the cream almost entirely reduced. Finish with a little butter, a few drops of lemon juice and enough warm Sauce à la Crème to coat.

Variation

Sauce à la Crème is the base for ***Sauce Ecossaise*** which is used to accompany eggs and poultry. Prepare a *brunoise* of 15 g (½ oz) each of celery, carrot, onion, and French beans. Place in a pan with a little butter and 50 ml (2 fl oz) Fonds Blanc, page 10, and stew until almost dry. Stir this into 600 ml (1 pint) Sauce à la Crème and warm gently.

MAKES APPROXIMATELY 600 ML (1 PINT)

Sauce aux Crevettes

500 ml (18 fl oz) Sauce Velouté de Poisson, page 28
65 ml (2½ fl oz) double cream
65 ml (2½ fl oz) Fumet de Poisson, page 13
50 g (2 oz) Beurre de Crevettes, page 103
15 g (½ oz) Beurre Colorant Rouge, page 101
2 tablespoons shelled, cooked shrimps
cayenne pepper

*P*lace the Sauce Velouté in a pan with the cream and Fumet de Poisson. Bring to the boil and cook briskly for 7–8 minutes, stirring continuously. Remove from the heat and add both of the compound butters to give a shell pink colour. Finish with the cooked shrimps and season lightly with cayenne pepper.

Uses

This sauce can be used with certain egg dishes. For **Oeufs aux Crevettes**, fill cooked tartlet cases with cooked shrimps mixed with the sauce. Place a poached or soft-boiled egg on top of each tartlet and coat with a little more of the sauce. Decorate each tartlet with four nice shelled shrimps. Alternatively, prepare a dish of scrambled egg and place a bouquet of cooked shrimps in the centre. Coat the shrimps with Sauce aux Crevettes and pour a *cordon* of the sauce around the eggs.

The '**Montreuil**' garnish for fish consists of plain boiled potatoes coated in Sauce aux Crevettes, surrounding the chosen fish coated in Sauce Vin Blanc.

Variation

The Velouté de Poisson used in the sauce may be replaced with Sauce Béchamel, page 30, for a subtler flavour.

MAKES APPROXIMATELY 500 ML (18 FL OZ)

Sauce Currie à l'Indienne

15 g ($\frac{1}{2}$ oz) butter
50 g (2 oz) onion, peeled and finely sliced
1 bouquet garni, comprising parsley stalks, thyme, $\frac{1}{2}$ bay leaf,
and a small piece each of mace and cinnamon
$\frac{1}{2}$–1 teaspoon curry powder
275 ml (9 fl oz) coconut milk
275 ml (9 fl oz) either Sauce Velouté or Sauce Velouté
de Poisson, page 28, according to whether the sauce is to
accompany meat or fish
100 ml (3$\frac{1}{2}$ fl oz) cream
a few drops lemon juice

*H*eat the butter in a small pan and cook the sliced onion together with the bouquet garni without allowing the onion to colour. Sprinkle in the curry powder and cook for 1 minute, then moisten with the coconut milk. Add the appropriate Sauce Velouté and simmer gently for 15 minutes. Pass through a fine strainer and finish with the cream and a few drops of lemon juice.

The coconut milk used in this recipe can be obtained by soaking 350 g (12 oz) freshly and finely grated coconut in 250 ml (8 fl oz) of lukewarm milk. Strain by squeezing firmly through a cloth.

Uses
This sauce is suitable for serving with egg, fish, shellfish and various poultry dishes.

Variation
If coconut milk is unavailable it can be replaced with an equal quantity of almond milk.

MAKES APPROXIMATELY 600 ML (1 PINT)

Sauce Diplomate

500 ml (18 fl oz) Sauce Normande, page 72
40 g (1½ oz) Beurre de Homard, page 103
1 tablespoon finely diced cooked lobster
½ tablespoon finely diced truffle

Heat the Sauce Normande gently, then finish at the last moment with the Beurre de Homard, the finely diced cooked lobster and the finely diced truffle.

Uses
Generally this sauce is served with whole, large poached fish, such as salmon or turbot.

Variations
Extra flavour may be given to the sauce by the addition of 1 tablespoon of brandy and/or a pinch of cayenne pepper. For **Sauce Riche**, also suitable for serving with whole poached fish, add 50 ml (2 fl oz) Essence de Truffes, page 17, and a further 40 g (1½ oz) of finely diced truffle.

MAKES APPROXIMATELY 500 ML (18 FL OZ)

Sauce Hollandaise

2 tablespoons wine vinegar
5 tablespoons water
salt
coarsely ground pepper
5 egg yolks
450 g (1 lb) unsalted butter, softened or melted
a few drops lemon juice

*P*lace the vinegar with 4 tablespoons water in a pan with a pinch each of salt and pepper. Reduce by two-thirds and transfer to a *bain-marie*.

Add another tablespoon water and the egg yolks to the reduction and whisk continuously over a gentle heat, while very gradually adding the butter. (It is important that the water in the *bain-marie* is kept just simmering throughout the process and that the whisking is brisk and thorough.) The sauce will thicken as the temperature rises and the yolks are cooked, but great care should be taken that the mixture does not overheat or it will separate. Add a few drops of water from time to time so as to ensure the sauce remains light.

Check the seasoning and add a few drops of lemon juice. Pass through a fine strainer and keep at a lukewarm temperature until the sauce is required, to prevent it from separating.

Uses

This delicious sauce is well known as an accompaniment for asparagus and poached salmon, but can be served, with equal success, with boiled cod, poached pike and trout.

Variation

To the above recipe add the juice of 1 blood orange together with a pinch of its grated zest for **Sauce Maltaise**.

MAKES APPROXIMATELY 500 ML (18 FL OZ)

Sauce Hongroise

65 g (2½ oz) butter
50 g (2 oz) onion, peeled and chopped
1 pinch salt
paprika
500 ml (18 fl oz) Sauce Velouté, page 28

Melt 25 g (1 oz) butter and gently cook the onion, without colouring. Season lightly with salt and paprika, then add the Sauce Velouté and simmer for a few minutes. Pass through a fine strainer and finish with the remaining butter. The resulting sauce should be a delicate pink colour, due to the paprika.

Uses

This lightly flavoured and coloured Velouté sauce makes an excellent accompaniment for noisettes of lamb and veal, eggs, poultry and fish. A great favourite is **Poularde à la Hongroise**: take a plump chicken and place it on a bed of root vegetables and herbs in a heavy casserole dish. Pour over a generous amount of melted butter, cover and set to cook in a moderate oven (180°C, 350°F, Gas Mark 4), basting frequently. When the bird is cooked, place on a dish and coat with Sauce Hongroise. Usually the chicken is surrounded with small mounds of rice pilaff containing diced tomato. As a general rule, dishes designated '**à la Hongroise**' include paprika and diced tomato, though not all require Sauce Hongroise specifically as an accompaniment.

Variation

When Sauce Hongroise is served with fish, such as poached fillets of flat, white fish, the Sauce Velouté should be substituted by Sauce Velouté de Poisson, page 28.

MAKES APPROXIMATELY 500 ML (18 FL OZ)

Sauce Mornay

500 ml (18 fl oz) Sauce Béchamel, page 30
100 ml (3½ fl oz) milk
15 g (½ oz) Gruyère cheese, grated
15 g (½ oz) Parmesan cheese, grated
25 g (1 oz) butter

Heat the Sauce Béchamel and stir in the milk. Reduce by a third and add all the grated cheese. Reheat for a few seconds, mix well to ensure that the cheese is melted, and finish with the butter.

Uses

Sauce Mornay is an extremely versatile though rather under-rated sauce. Care should be taken to use the correct cheeses, and freshly grated Parmesan will taste much better than a ready-grated version. Vegetables such as cauliflower, Brussels sprouts and root fennel can be coated with the sauce, sprinkled with grated Parmesan and fine dried breadcrumbs then browned under the grill to be served '*au Gratin*'. Sauce Mornay can be used for many hors d'oeuvre tartlets. Fillings such as poached roe, seafood or mushrooms are usually placed in the pastry case then coated with the sauce before being glazed under the grill.

For an '*à la Florentine*' garnish for fish, blanch and stew 250 g (9 oz) of spinach, then place it in a dish. Position the chosen poached fish on top, then coat with Sauce Mornay (see the variation below) and glaze under the grill.

Variation

If the sauce is to coat or accompany fish, replace the milk with an equal quantity of poaching liquid from the fish before proceeding as above.

MAKES APPROXIMATELY 500 ML (18 FL OZ)

Sauce Mousseuse

250 g (9 oz) butter, beaten until very soft and creamy
1 pinch salt
1 scant tablespoon lemon juice
200 ml (7 fl oz) water
2 tablespoons double cream, well whipped

Scald a small pan by immersing it in boiling water, then wipe it clean and dry. Place the butter and salt in the pan and beat in the lemon juice. Gradually whisk in the water and finish at the last moment with the whipped cream.

Uses

This preparation, although classified as a sauce, is more of a compound butter, and is suitable for serving with boiled fish. Serve the sauce at room temperature; the heat of the fish should be sufficient to melt the sauce. Sauce Mousseuse may also be served in place of melted butter with delicately flavoured vegetables such as asparagus and artichokes.

MAKES APPROXIMATELY 450 ML ($\frac{3}{4}$ PINT)

Sauce Nantua

500 ml (18 fl oz) Sauce Béchamel, page 30
150 ml (¼ pint) double cream
65 g (2½ oz) Beurre d'Ecrevisse, page 103
10 small cooked crayfish tails, shelled

Combine the Sauce Béchamel with half of the cream and reduce by one-third. Pass through a fine strainer and adjust the consistency by adding the rest of the cream. Finish with the Beurre d'Ecrevisse and the crayfish tails.

Uses

This sauce can be used with a number of small egg dishes that also contain some form of shellfish. For **Oeufs Daumont**, cook large field mushrooms in butter and garnish with finely diced crayfish tails mixed with Sauce Nantua. Top each mushroom with a poached egg coated with more of the sauce and garnish with slices of truffle. Sauce Nantua is used for other dishes designated '**Daumont**', and always accompanies items which have the classic '**Daumont**' garnish. For this garnish for cooked fish use 10 large mushrooms cooked in butter, containing halved crayfish tails bound in Sauce Nantua; 10 small quenelles made from fish and cream forcemeat; 10 thick slices of soft roe, egg-and-breadcrumbed then deep fried, and accompany the whole with more Sauce Nantua.

On its own the sauce is usually served with whole or large cuts of fish, such as salmon, whiting or stuffed sole.

Variations

A dash of brandy can be added to the reduction if liked, or the sauce can be seasoned with a touch of cayenne pepper.

MAKES APPROXIMATELY 500 ML (18 FL OZ)

Sauce Newburg

750 g–1 kg (1½–2 lb) raw lobster, recently killed and washed
50 g (2 oz) butter
85 ml (3 fl oz) oil
salt
cayenne pepper
2 tablespoons brandy
200 ml (7 fl oz) Marsala or Malmsey Madeira
200 ml (7 fl oz) double cream
200 ml (7 fl oz) Fumet de Poisson, page 13

*T*ake the lobster and cut the tail into sections; remove the claws and crack them. Split the carapace lengthways and discard the sac (located near the top of the head). Remove the creamy parts and coral from the head and pound with half of the butter. Reserve this for use later. Heat the oil with the rest of the butter and add the pieces of lobster. Season with salt and cayenne pepper and fry on all sides until bright red. Drain off the fat and flame with brandy (warm the brandy, set alight and pour immediately into the pan), then add the Marsala or Madeira. Reduce by two-thirds, then moisten with the cream and fish stock and simmer for 25 minutes. Strain.

Remove the flesh from the lobster pieces and cut into small dice. Finish the sauce by adding the reserved creamy paste and boiling gently to cook. Just before serving add the diced lobster flesh and check the seasoning.

Uses

The dish known as **Homard Newburg** can be made by preparing the sauce as above. However, instead of dicing the flesh, it should be cut into neat thick slices and placed in a *timbale* before being coated with sauce. A border of pommes de terre duchesse may be piped around the dish and lightly glazed in the oven beforehand.

MAKES APPROXIMATELY 600 ML (1 PINT)

Sauce Normande

3 egg yolks
150 ml (¼ pint) double cream
350 ml (12 fl oz) Sauce Velouté de Poisson, page 28
50 ml (2 fl oz) Cuisson de Champignons, page 17
50 ml (2 fl oz) cooking liquor from mussels
100 ml (3½ fl oz) Fumet de Poisson, page 13
a squeeze lemon juice
65 g (2½ oz) butter

Combine the egg yolks with 50 ml (2 fl oz) of the cream and place in a pan with the Sauce Velouté, the Cuisson de Champignons, mussel cooking liquor, Fumet de Poisson and lemon juice. Stir well together and bring to the boil. Allow the sauce to reduce by one-third, stirring continuously, then pass through a fine strainer. Finish the sauce with the remaining cream and the butter. Check the seasoning.

Uses

This creamy fish sauce makes an excellent accompaniment for poached white fish, especially sole. The Fumet de Poisson should be based on trimmings of the fish in preparation.

MAKES APPROXIMATELY 500 ML (18 FL OZ)

Sauce Régence

100 ml (3½ fl oz) dry white wine
100 ml (3½ fl oz) Fumet de Poisson, page 13
15 g (½ oz) mushroom trimmings
15 g (½ oz) truffle trimmings
400 ml (14 fl oz) Sauce Normande, opposite
1 tablespoon Essence de Truffes, page 17

*P*lace the wine and Fumet de Poisson in a pan with the mushroom and truffle trimmings and reduce by half. Strain through a clean cloth and add to the Sauce Normande. Simmer gently for 5 minutes, then finish with the truffle essence.

Uses

This is suitable for serving with a wide range of fish, particularly those garnished in the '*Régence*' manner (with quenelles of forcemeat made from whiting and Beurre d'Ecrevisse, page 103; poached and bearded oysters; sautéed button mushrooms; truffles cut into olive shapes; and slices of poached soft roe). A marvellous example of this is *Saumon Régence*: stuff a whole salmon with forcemeat made from whiting and poach or braise as normal. Place on a platter edged with piped pommes de terre marquise (duchesse potatoes containing tomato purée) and surround the fish with bouquets of the garnish ingredients. Stick three decorative skewers in the fish, each garnished with a cooked crayfish, quenelle and glazed truffle. Serve Sauce Régence separately.

Variations

A *Sauce Régence for Poultry* can be made as above but replacing the fish stock with Cuisson de Champignons, page 17, and using Sauce Allemande, page 53, instead of Sauce Normande.

MAKES APPROXIMATELY 500 ML (18 FL OZ)

Sauce Smitane

25 g (1 oz) butter
50 g (2 oz) onion, peeled and finely chopped
100 ml (3½ fl oz) dry white wine
300 ml (½ pint) sour cream
a few drops lemon juice

Stew the onion in the butter until lightly coloured, then add the wine and reduce until almost entirely evaporated. Add the sour cream and simmer gently for 5 minutes. Finish with the lemon juice to give a good tangy flavour. Season to taste and pass through a fine strainer to finish.

Uses

This simple sauce makes an ideal accompaniment for game such as pheasant, partridge or quail cooked '**en Casserole**' or '**en Cocotte**'. For this method of cooking, flameproof dishes are used and the food is served from the dish at the table. First the birds should be put into the covered dish with a quantity of melted butter: place in a hot oven (220°C, 425°F, Gas Mark 7) and cook, basting frequently. When the birds are ready, remove from the dish, add a spoonful or two of Fonds Blanc, page 10, and of brandy and allow to boil and reduce. Skim, then return the birds to the dish. Replace the lid until required. (This is the '**en Casserole**' version. The birds may also be served with button onions cooked in butter, small cooked mushrooms and olive-shaped truffles or potatoes for the '**en Cocotte**' version.) Serve with a sauceboat of Sauce Smitane. Small items of sautéed game, such as fillet of venison or jointed plump, young pheasant may also be accompanied with this sauce.

MAKES APPROXIMATELY 300 ML (½ PINT)

Sauce Soubise

250 g (9 oz) onions, peeled and sliced
65 g (2½ oz) butter
300 ml (½ pint) thick Sauce Béchamel, page 30
salt
ground white pepper
caster sugar
50 ml (2 fl oz) double cream

Blanch the onions in boiling water, drain thoroughly and stew gently in 25 g (1 oz) butter until soft but not coloured. Add the Sauce Béchamel and season with a pinch each of salt, pepper and caster sugar. Transfer to a casserole, cover and place in the centre of a moderate oven (160°C, 325°F, Gas Mark 3). Allow to cook gently for 45 minutes, stirring occasionally and lowering the heat if the sauce begins to colour.

Pass through a sieve and reheat, finishing with the remaining butter and the cream.

Uses

This smooth white sauce is also known as ***Coulis d'Oignons Soubise*** and has a variety of uses. It may be served with egg cutlets (chopped hard-boiled egg bound together with thick Sauce Béchamel and raw egg, then egg-and-breadcrumbed and deep fried), roast fillet of beef, grilled oxtail and braised ox tongue. For ***Côte de Veau Orloff***, a thick Sauce Soubise is used to stuff shallow fried veal cutlets. A slice of truffle may be slipped in with the sauce and then the cutlets should be reshaped. Coat first with Sauce Soubise, then with Sauce Mornay, page 68, and glaze quickly under the grill.

Variation

Sauce Soubise Tomatée is made by adding 150 ml (¼ pint) fresh tomato purée to the basic sauce to finish.

MAKES APPROXIMATELY 450 ML (¾ PINT)

Sauce Tyrolienne

100 ml (3½ fl oz) dry white wine
100 ml (3½ fl oz) tarragon vinegar
2 tablespoons chopped shallot
6 peppercorns, crushed
2 tablespoons chopped fresh tarragon
1 tablespoon chopped fresh chervil
50 g (2 oz) well-reduced fresh tomato purée
4 egg yolks
250 ml (9 fl oz) oil
cayenne pepper

*P*lace the wine and vinegar in a small pan with the shallot, peppercorns and herbs. Bring to the boil and reduce by three-quarters. Allow to cool, then squeeze through a cloth, twisting firmly. Return to the pan. Add the tomato purée and the egg yolks. Whisk over a gentle heat, then add the oil as for making Mayonnaise, page 85, drop by drop to begin with and then in a thin stream as the sauce thickens. Correct the seasoning and finish with a hint of cayenne pepper. Do not allow the sauce to become more than lukewarm.

Uses
This sauce makes an excellent accompaniment for grilled fish and meat. In combination with 250 g (9 oz) each of floured, deep-fried onion rings and chopped tomato flesh, cooked in butter, the sauce forms the '*à la Tyrolienne*' garnish.

Variation
A variation of this sauce suited for serving with fish is **Sauce Véron**: to 120 ml (4 fl oz) of the above sauce, add 300 ml (½ pint) Sauce Normande, page 72, and finish with 1 tablespoon melted Glace de Viande, page 16, and 1½ teaspoons anchovy essence.

MAKES APPROXIMATELY 450 ML (¾ PINT)

Sauce Vénitienne

200 ml (7 fl oz) tarragon vinegar
25 g (1 oz) shallot, peeled and chopped
15 g (½ oz) fresh chervil
400 ml (14 fl oz) Sauce Vin Blanc, page 79
50 g (2 oz) Beurre Colorant Vert, page 102
1 tablespoon chopped mixed fresh chervil and tarragon

*P*lace the vinegar, shallot and chervil in a pan and reduce by two-thirds. Squeeze the reduction through muslin, then add it to the Sauce Vin Blanc. Finish with the Beurre Colorant Vert and mixed herbs to give a soft green colour.

Uses
This sauce is served with various preparations of fish, particularly salmon and pike poached in Court-bouillon au Vinaigre, page 21

Variation
Sauce Vénitienne may also be used to accompany poultry and egg dishes. In this case substitute Sauce Allemande, page 53, for the Sauce Vin Blanc and proceed as above.

MAKES APPROXIMATELY 475 ML (16 FL OZ)

Sauce Villeroy

150 ml (¼ pint) Fonds Blanc, page 10, flavoured with
a knuckle of ham
500 ml (18 fl oz) Sauce Allemande, page 53
2 tablespoons Essence de Truffes, page 17

R educe the Fonds Blanc until only 2 tablespoons are left, then add the Sauce Allemande and Essence de Truffes. Reduce rapidly, stirring constantly until a thick, coating consistency is reached. Allow to cool slightly before use.

Uses

This sauce is only used to coat items of food which are then egg-and-breadcrumbed and deep fried. These dishes are always designated '*à la Villeroy*' and are usually served as an hors d'oeuvre. For **Attereaux d'Huîtres à la Villeroy**, poach 6 large oysters per person, beard them then thread onto wooden skewers, alternating with slices of cooked mushroom. Coat first with Sauce Villeroy which has had the juices from the oysters added to the reduction, then in egg and breadcrumbs. Mould into cylinder shapes and deep fry until golden brown. For **Beignets de Laitances Villeroy**, the Sauce Villeroy should be very thick and contain 1 tablespoon of diced truffle. Poach some soft roes in Court-bouillon au Vin Blanc, page 20, drain, cool then coat with the sauce. When cold, dip into a light batter and deep fry. Serve on a serviette and surround with crisply fried sprigs of parsley.

Variation

Sauce Villeroy Soubisée is made by reducing 500 ml (18 fl oz) Sauce Allemande with 200 ml (7 fl oz) Sauce Soubise, page 75, until a coating consistency is attained. This sauce has similar uses to the basic sauce and may, if desired, be finished with diced truffle.

MAKES APPROXIMATELY 300 ML (½ PINT)

Sauce Vin Blanc

500 ml (18 fl oz) Sauce Velouté de Poisson, page 28
100 ml (3½ fl oz) Fumet de Poisson, page 13
2 egg yolks
65 g (2½ oz) butter

*P*lace the Sauce Velouté in a pan with the Fumet de Poisson and simmer gently. Add the egg yolks and reduce by one-third whilst stirring continuously. Finish the sauce, away from the heat, with the butter.

Uses

This fine sauce is excellent served with cutlets of salmon or poached fillets of sole, as well as other fish preparations. It is particularly suitable for fish dishes which require glazing. The '*à la Dieppoise*' garnish for fish dishes uses Sauce Vin Blanc with an addition of reduced cooking liquor from the fish in preparation, as well as 100 g (3½ oz) shelled prawns, and 30 mussels poached in white wine, shelled and bearded.

Variations

There are two other methods of making Sauce Vin Blanc; both have a milder fish flavour than the recipe given above. Place 40 ml (1½ fl oz) Fumet de Poisson in a pan and reduce by half; add 3 egg yolks, then make the sauce by whisking in 250 g (9 oz) melted butter in the same way as for Sauce Hollandaise, page 66. Alternatively, place 3 egg yolks in pan and warm gently whilst whisking. Gradually add 250 g (9 oz) melted butter and finish by adding 40 ml (1½ fl oz) Fumet de Poisson.

Sauce Saint-Malo, which is excellent with grilled saltwater fish, has Sauce Vin Blanc as its foundation and any of the above methods may be used. To 500 ml (18 fl oz) Sauce Vin Blanc add 25 g (1 oz) Beurre d'Echalote, page 102, 1 teaspoon made mustard and a few drops of anchovy essence.

MAKES APPROXIMATELY 500 ML (18 FL OZ)

COLD SAUCES & ASPIC JELLIES

Sauces Froides et Gelées

*T*he cold sauces found in this chapter are among the most useful of all sauces to have in your repertoire. Sauce Mayonnaise, for example, provides not only a pleasant sauce in its own right but a springboard to a wide range of variations. By adding herbs, purées, infusions and chopped delicacies the basic sauce can be altered to suit most hors d'oeuvre and cold entrées.

Cold items such as hams and poached salmon are always popular features for a buffet table and can look truly spectacular when presented beautifully decorated and glazed with aspic jelly. Recipes for stocks and clarification procedures for a number of different aspic jellies are given at the end of the chapter.

Aïoli de Provence

30 g (1 oz) garlic cloves, peeled
1 egg yolk
salt
275 ml (9 fl oz) olive oil
juice of 1 lemon
½ tablespoon water

C rush the garlic, then pound to a smooth consistency in a mortar. Add the egg yolk with a pinch of salt and gradually mix in the oil, allowing it to fall drop by drop to begin with, then faster – in a thin stream – as the sauce thickens. Work the sauce vigorously with the pestle throughout the process. The consistency of the sauce should be adjusted as you proceed by adding the lemon juice and cold water a little at a time.

Should the sauce separate, it can be reconstituted by working it back into a fresh egg yolk as for Sauce Mayonnaise, page 85.

Uses

This pungent sauce can be used in the preparation of simple hors d'oeuvre or can be served as a dip accompanied by a selection of raw carrot, celery, cauliflower, and other vegetables, trimmed into short sticks or florets. It can also be spooned on to halves of baked jacket potatoes as barbecue fare.

Variations

A quick method for making a similar sauce is to add some smooth puréed garlic (this is available commercially) to ready-made Sauce Mayonnaise, page 85. A milder flavour can be obtained by first simmering the cloves of peeled garlic in milk until soft, before crushing or pounding to a purée.

MAKES APPROXIMATELY 400 ML (14 FL OZ)

Sauce Génoise

*25 g (1 oz) each fresh parsley, chervil, tarragon, chives
and young salad burnet
20 g (¾ oz) freshly skinned pistachio nuts
15 g (½ oz) pine nuts
1–2 teaspoons cold Sauce Béchamel, page 30
3 egg yolks
salt
pepper
juice of 1 lemon
500 ml (18 fl oz) oil*

*B*lanch the herbs in boiling water for 2 minutes, then drain, refresh and pass through a fine sieve to form a purée. Reserve this for later use.

Place the pistachio and pine nuts in a liquidizer or mortar and work to a smooth paste with 1–2 teaspoons of cold Sauce Béchamel. Pass through a fine sieve and place in a basin with the egg yolks. Season with salt and pepper and a few drops of lemon juice. Whisk briskly and begin to add the oil drop by drop. When the sauce begins to thicken, pour in the oil in a thin stream, whisking quickly all the time. Maintain a smooth consistency by occasionally adding a few drops of lemon juice.

When all the oil has been incorporated, sharpen with lemon juice and stir in the puréed herbs. Check the seasoning. Cover with greaseproof paper or cling film if not for immediate use.

Uses
This is usually served as an accompaniment for cold fish such as salmon, trout and turbot.

Variation
If pine nuts are not available, replace with an equal quantity of blanched sweet almonds.

MAKES APPROXIMATELY 600 ML (1 PINT)

Sauce Gribiche

3 hard-boiled eggs, shelled
½ teaspoon made English mustard
salt
pepper
275 ml (9 fl oz) oil
2 teaspoons vinegar
50 g (2 oz) mixed capers and gherkins, chopped
½ tablespoon mixed chopped fresh parsley, tarragon and chervil

*H*alve the eggs and place the yolks in a basin. Crush them and work to a smooth paste with the mustard and a pinch each of salt and pepper. Proceed in the same way as for Sauce Mayonnaise, page 85, by gradually adding the oil and vinegar. Finish the sauce with the chopped capers, gherkins and herbs and half of the reserved egg white cut into short *julienne*.

Uses
Serve this piquant sauce with cold cutlets of salmon or fillets of trout, or any other type of cold fish.

MAKES APPROXIMATELY 300 ML (½ PINT)

Sauce Groseilles au Raifort

50 ml (2 fl oz) port wine
1 pinch grated nutmeg
1 pinch ground cinnamon
salt
pepper
200 g (7 oz) redcurrant jelly, melted
1 tablespoon finely grated horseradish

*P*our the port wine into a small pan and add the nutmeg, cinnamon, salt and pepper. Bring to the boil and reduce by one-third. Mix in the melted redcurrant jelly and grated horseradish and stir occasionally until cold.

Uses
This sauce is suitable for serving with joints of marinated game and beef or with cold beef, duck and venison.

Variations
Freshly grated horseradish has a most distinctive flavour and is more familiar used in a cream sauce to accompany roast beef. To make **Sauce Raifort**, mix equal quantities of grated horse-radish and fresh breadcrumbs and soak them in milk. Drain and squeeze, then add lightly whipped cream to give a soft consistency. Sharpen with vinegar and season with salt and pepper. This can also accompany smoked trout and mackerel and cold roast beef. For **Sauce Raifort aux Noix**, mix 100 g (4 oz) each grated horseradish and skinned, chopped walnuts. Sweeten with a teaspoon of sugar and fold into 150 ml ($\frac{1}{4}$ pint) whipped double cream. Serve this with cold trout or char.
MAKES APPROXIMATELY 250 ML (8 FL OZ)

Sauce Mayonnaise

2 egg yolks
salt
white pepper
½ tablespoon wine vinegar
300 ml (½ pint) oil
2 tablespoons boiling water

Whisk the yolks in a basin with a good pinch of salt, a pinch of pepper and a little of the vinegar. Add and whisk in the oil, drop by drop to begin with, then faster in a stream, as the sauce begins to thicken. Adjust the consistency occasionally by adding a few more drops of vinegar. Lastly, add the boiling water, which ensures that the emulsification holds, even if the sauce is not used immediately.

The oil used in making Mayonnaise should be at room temperature. If the oil is too cold, or if it is added too quickly the sauce may separate. To restore a curdled Mayonnaise, place another egg yolk in a clean basin with a little vinegar and whisk in oil, drop by drop until it begins to thicken. Slowly pour the separated Mayonnaise in whilst whisking vigorously.

Uses
Many composed cold sauces are derived from Mayonnaise. It can also be served, in its original form, with almost all cold fish, meat, egg and vegetable dishes.

Variations
If a very white Mayonnaise is required the vinegar should be replaced with lemon juice, which will also give a pleasant flavour. Usually it is best to use good quality olive oil or sunflower oil, but a small amount of walnut or grape seed oil can be used to make up the correct quantity. These oils have strong, nutty flavours and will alter the character of the sauce.

MAKES APPROXIMATELY 300 ML (½ PINT)

Sauce Moutarde à la Crème

20 g (¾ oz) English mustard powder
salt
pepper
a few drops lemon juice
200 ml (7 fl oz) very fresh double cream

*P*lace the mustard in a basin, season with salt and pepper and sharpen with lemon juice. Add the cream, drop by drop as if making Mayonnaise, page 85, stirring or whisking all the time.

Uses

This is used in the preparation of various hors d'oeuvres. Poached, shelled mussels are delicious mixed with finely sliced celery and Sauce Moutarde à la Crème, then flavoured with pepper. To serve cauliflower as an hors d'oeuvre, cook briefly in salted water, drain and marinate in oil and vinegar, then coat with the above sauce.

Variation

A fine *julienne* of celery may be added to the finished sauce, which gives a pleasant crunchiness.

MAKES APPROXIMATELY 300 ML (½ PINT)

Sauce Suédoise

250 g (9 oz) cooking apples, peeled, cored and sliced
2–3 tablespoons white wine
350 ml (12 fl oz) thick Sauce Mayonnaise, page 85
2 teaspoons grated horseradish

*P*lace the sliced apples and wine in a pan with a tightly fitting lid. Cover and cook gently until the apples are very soft, shaking the pan occasionally to prevent burning. Pass through a fine sieve and return the purée to a clean pan. Reduce over a moderate heat, stirring continuously, until you have approximately 120 ml (4 fl oz) of thick purée. Cool, then chill before blending with the Mayonnaise. Finish the sauce with the grated horseradish.

Uses
This distinctive sauce makes an excellent accompaniment for cold roast goose and pork.

Variations
If sweet apples are used, acidulate the purée with a few drops of lemon juice to achieve the correct tartness. Alternatively, puréed whitecurrants or green gooseberries may be used. As these fruits have strong flavours, reduce the amount of purée to 65 ml ($2\frac{1}{2}$ fl oz). A touch of English mustard powder may be added to any of these variations of the sauce.

MAKES APPROXIMATELY 475 ML (16 FL OZ)

Sauce Tartare

2 hard-boiled egg yolks
salt
pepper
250 ml (8 fl oz) oil
1 tablespoon vinegar
2 young spring onions or a few chives
2 teaspoons Sauce Mayonnaise, page 85

Crush the yolks in a basin and work to a smooth paste with a pinch each of salt and pepper. Gradually add the oil and vinegar as for making Sauce Mayonnaise, page 85.

Pound the spring onions or chives with the Mayonnaise. Pass through a fine sieve and add to the prepared sauce.

Uses

This sauce is suitable for serving with cold fish and shellfish, cold meat and poultry. It can also be served with meat and poultry cooked '*à la Diable*' such as Poulet de Grains Grillé Diable, page 38, and shallow fried fillets of fish.

Variation

Sauce Tartare may also be finished with 15 g ($\frac{1}{2}$ oz) finely chopped capers, 25 g (1 oz) finely chopped gherkins and 2 teaspoons finely chopped *fines herbes*.

MAKES APPROXIMATELY 275 ML (9 FL OZ)

Sauce Verte

25 g (1 oz) each spinach and watercress leaves
25 g (1 oz) mixed sprigs fresh parsley, tarragon and chervil
350 ml (12 fl oz) thick Sauce Mayonnaise, page 85
salt
white pepper

*P*lunge the spinach, watercress and herbs into boiling water and blanch for 5 minutes. Refresh quickly by placing them in a sieve under cold running water; this will help to preserve their bright green colour. Squeeze out all the water, then pound the leaves and squeeze firmly through a clean cloth to produce a thick herb juice. Add this to the thick Mayonnaise and season well with salt and pepper.

Uses
This is suitable for serving with cold shellfish and fish such as poached salmon trout set in clarified Gelée de Poisson, pages 95 and 97. As with any Mayonnaise-based sauce, Sauce Verte can be thinned with a little boiling water to give a coating consistency. This can be used to coat small filled tartlets, cold stuffed eggs, and so on. It should be noted, however, that it is generally more correct to use one of the Chaud-froid sauces, pages 37, 59 and 60, for this purpose.

Variations
A few chives may be added to the list of herbs above and the sauce may also be finished with a squeeze of lemon juice to give a tangy flavour. Another coloured Mayonnaise, useful for accompanying hors d'oeuvre and cold entrées is **Sauce Andalouse**: to 350 ml (12 fl oz) fairly thick Sauce Mayonnaise, add 135 ml (4½ fl oz) very smooth bright red fresh tomato purée or 2 tablespoons commercial tomato purée, and 25 g (1 oz) red pepper cut into small dice.

MAKES APPROXIMATELY 400 ML (14 FL OZ)

Sauce Vinaigrette

275 ml (9 fl oz) oil, preferably olive oil
100 ml (3½ fl oz) wine vinegar
1 tablespoon small capers
1 tablespoon chopped fresh parsley
20 g (¾ oz) mixed chopped fresh tarragon, chervil and chives
40 g (1½ oz) onion, peeled and finely chopped
good pinch each salt and coarsely ground pepper

Mix all the ingredients together well, either by whisking them or placing them in screwtop jar and shaking until the oil droplets are perfectly suspended in the vinegar and the sauce is cloudy in appearance.

Uses

This sauce is also known as **Sauce Ravigote**. It can be served with various tossed salads in which case the salad should be prepared and chilled lightly, then tossed with the freshly made sauce just before serving. Other vegetables to be served cold such as diced potato and cauliflower florets can be blanched or cooked until tender, then immediately tossed in the sauce. Allow to cool, then chill – thus using the sauce as a type of marinade. Traditionally Sauce Vinaigrette accompanies calf's head, calf's feet, pig's and sheep's trotters, and similar dishes.

Variations

1 finely chopped clove garlic and/or 1 teaspoon of Dijon mustard may be added to the ingredients above. Red or white wine vinegar can be used according to the main item of food to be accompanied by the sauce. The sauce may be made in advance and stored in a covered container in the refrigerator, but the herbs or garlic should only be added just before use.

MAKES APPROXIMATELY 400 ML (14 FL OZ)

Sauce Vincent

50 g (2 oz) mixed fresh sorrel, parsley, tarragon, chervil,
chives and salad burnet, in equal quantities
25 g (1 oz) watercress leaves
25 g (1 oz) spinach leaves
3 freshly cooked hard-boiled egg yolks
3 small raw egg yolks
400 ml (14 fl oz) oil
½–1½ tablespoons wine vinegar
1–2 tablespoons Derby sauce

*B*lanch the herbs and leaves in boiling water for 2–3 minutes. Drain well, refresh and squeeze out all the water. Place in a bowl with the hard-boiled egg yolks and pound until smooth. Sieve finely and place in a basin with the raw egg yolks and seasoning. Proceed as for Sauce Mayonnaise, page 85, by adding the oil and thinning with vinegar as necessary. Finish with Derby sauce to taste.

Uses
This sauce is suitable for serving with cold fish and shellfish.
MAKES APPROXIMATELY 450 ML (¾ PINT)

Fonds pour Gelée Ordinaire

1 kg (2 lb) knuckle and shin of veal
700 g (1½ lb) round piece of shank of beef
700 g (1½ lb) veal bones, chopped into small pieces
100 g (4 oz) carrots, peeled and roughly chopped
100 g (4 oz) onions, peeled and roughly chopped
25 g (1 oz) leek, sliced
25 g (1 oz) celery, sliced
6 tablespoons clean fat, such as strained dripping
2 calf's feet, blanched and boned
125 g (4½ oz) fresh pork rind
1 small bouquet garni
4.5 litres (8 pints) water

*B*one out the meats and break the bones into small, evenly sized pieces. Brown all the bones in the oven, then place in a stockpot. Fry the vegetables in half of the fat until light brown, then add to the bones with the calf's foot, pork rind and bouquet garni. Pour in the cold water. Bring to the boil, skim and simmer gently for 4–5 hours, adding more water if necessary to maintain the liquid level throughout.

Cut the beef and veal into large dice and brown lightly in the remaining fat. Place in another pan, cover with some of the prepared stock and boil until it is reduced to a glaze. Repeat this process 2 or 3 times. Add the rest of the stock, bring to the boil, skim off all the fat and simmer gently until all the flavour has been extracted from the meat. Top up the pan with boiling water so as to maintain a liquid level of approximately 2½ litres (4½ pints).

Strain to remove the flavouring ingredients, then pass through a fine hair sieve and allow to cool. Refrigerate overnight before clarifying (see page 96); this will make it possible to remove any fat from the surface and any sediment at the bottom.

MAKES APPROXIMATELY 2.5 LITRES (4½ PINTS)

Fonds pour Gelée de Volaille

700 g (1½ lb) knuckle of veal
700 g (1½ lb) shank of beef
450 g (1 lb) veal bones, broken into small pieces
700 g (1½ lb) chicken carcass, giblets and scalded legs
2 small calf's feet, blanched and boned
4 litres (7 pints) light Fonds Blanc, page 10
75 g (3 oz) carrot, peeled and roughly chopped
75 g (3 oz) onion, peeled and roughly chopped
25 g (1 oz) leek, sliced
25 g (1 oz) celery, sliced
1 small bouquet garni

*B*one the meat and chop the bones into small pieces. Place all the bones and meat in a stockpot with the calf's foot, cover with the stock and bring to the boil. Skim carefully, then add the vegetables and bouquet garni. Allow to simmer gently, uncovered, for 3 hours, skimming frequently and maintaining the level of liquid with stock or water for half of the cooking time. Add no more liquid during the last 1½ hours.

Strain to remove the flavouring ingredients, then pass through a fine hair sieve and allow to cool. Refrigerate overnight before clarifying; this will make it possible to remove any fat from the surface and any sediment at the bottom.

Uses

When clarified (see page 97) this aspic jelly can be used to coat cold joints or whole poultry. Cold poached poultry can also be coated first with Sauce Chaud-froid, page 59, and then decorated with red ox tongue and slices of truffle or trimmed vegetables, before applying a thin coating of the aspic jelly.

MAKES APPROXIMATELY 2.5 LITRES (4½ PINTS)

Fonds pour Gelée de Gibier

450 g (1 lb) knuckle of veal
1 kg (2 lb) shank of beef
6 tablespoons clean fat, such as strained dripping
375 g (13 oz) veal bones, cut into small pieces
1 kg (2 lb) trimmings and carcasses of game
100 g ($3\frac{1}{2}$ oz) carrot, peeled and sliced
100 g ($3\frac{1}{4}$ oz) onion, peeled and sliced
25 g (1 oz) leek, sliced
40 g ($1\frac{1}{2}$ oz) celery, sliced
2 small calf's feet
1 small bouquet garni, including thyme
3–4 juniper berries
4 litres (7 pints) water

Bone out the meat and break the bones into small pieces. Cut the meat into pieces and brown in the oven with half of the fat, all the bones and trimmings of game. Fry the vegetables in the remaining fat in a large stockpot. Add the browned meat, bones and trimmings. Deglaze the roasting pan with a little water and add to the pot with the calf's feet, bouquet garni and juniper berries. Pour in sufficient water just to cover, then bring to the boil and reduce to a syrupy glaze. Add the rest of the water, bring back to the boil, skim carefully and simmer gently for 3 hours. Pass through a fine strainer. Cool and re-frigerate overnight before clarifying; this will make it possible to remove any fat from the surface and any sediment at the bottom.

Uses
When clarified (see page 97) this aspic jelly can be used to coat small items of cold game such as pheasant, partridge or quail, which have previously been coated with Sauce Chaud-froid Brune, page 37.

MAKES APPROXIMATELY 2.5 LITRES ($4\frac{1}{2}$ PINTS)

Fonds pour Gelée de Poisson

375 g (13 oz) second quality fish such as gurnet, weever
and whiting
375 g (13 oz) bones and trimmings of sole
100 g (4 oz) onion, peeled and sliced
15 g ($\frac{1}{2}$ oz) parsley stalks
50 g (2 oz) mushroom trimmings
3 litres ($5\frac{1}{4}$ pints) light Fumet de Poisson, page 13

*P*lace the fish, bones and trimmings in a large pan with the onion, parsley stalks and mushroom trimmings. Cover with the Fumet de Poisson. Bring quickly to the boil and skim carefully. Simmer gently for 45 minutes, then pass through a fine strainer. Cool and refrigerate overnight before clarifying; this will make it possible to remove any fat from the surface and any sediment at the bottom.

Uses
This stock, when clarified as an aspic jelly (see page 97), is used to coat cold poached fish. Usually the fish is skinned after cooking and may be first coated with Sauce Chaud-froid for Fish, page 59.

MAKES APPROXIMATELY 2.5 LITRES (4$\frac{1}{2}$ PINTS)

Clarification de Gelée Ordinaire

450 g (1 lb) lean minced beef
2 egg whites
1 pinch each chopped fresh chervil and tarragon
1 litre (1¾ pints) Fonds pour Gelée Ordinaire, page 92, slightly warmed
up to 7 leaves of gelatine, soaked in cold water

*P*lace the minced beef, egg whites and herbs in a heavy bottomed pan, add the slightly warmed stock (which should be free of fat and sediment) and mix with a whisk to ensure a thorough distribution of the egg whites. Bring to the boil gently, keeping the bottom of the pan clean using a flat-ended spatula and taking great care that the jelly is disturbed as little as possible. Simmer very gently for 25 minutes without further stirring of any sort.

Put a little of the jelly in a saucer and place on ice or in a refrigerator to ascertain if it sets sufficiently. If not, add a few leaves of soaked gelatine to obtain a more definite set without it being in any way too firm. Simmer for a few minutes more then pass through a clean cloth and make sure that any traces of fat are removed. The resultant liquid jelly should be crystal clear.

Variations

If wine is to be added to the jelly this should be done when the jelly is almost cold. To ensure that the addition of wine at this final stage does not interfere with the set of the jelly, remember to allow for extra liquid when judging whether or not to use gelatine. Wines such as Madeira, sherry and Marsala should be added in the proportion of 100 ml (3½ fl oz) per 1 litre (1¾ pints) of jelly.

MAKES APPROXIMATELY 1 LITRE (1¾ PINTS)

Clarification des Gelées de Volaille, Gibier et Poisson

Gelée de Volaille

Follow the procedure for the clarification of Gelée Ordinaire, opposite, but replace half of the minced beef with an equal amount of chopped chicken necks, and use Fonds pour Gelée de Volaille, page 93, to provide the liquid content.

Gelée de Gibier

Follow the procedure for the clarification of Gelée Ordinaire, opposite, but replace half of the minced beef with an equal amount of minced game flesh, and use Fonds pour Gelée de Gibier, page 94, to provide the liquid content. For a specific flavour it is important that the minced game corresponds to the game with which the jelly will be served. All game jellies can be improved in flavour by the addition of 2 tablespoons of fine brandy per 1 litre ($1\frac{3}{4}$ pints) of jelly. Inferior brandy should not be used for this under any circumstances.

Gelée de Poisson

Use 2 egg whites and 50 g (2 oz) chopped whiting fillet per 1 litre ($1\frac{3}{4}$ pints) Fonds pour Gelée de Poisson, page 95. Pound the fish and mix with the egg white. Place in a pan and pour on the cold stock. Bring to the boil, mixing gently (see opposite), then simmer without stirring for 15 minutes. Pass through a clean cloth and reserve for use.

N.B. The remarks regarding the setting qualities of the stocks and the addition of wines given opposite apply to all these variations.

MAKES APPROXIMATELY 1 LITRE ($1\frac{3}{4}$ PINTS)

COMPOUND BUTTERS

Beurres Composés

*M*ost compound butters are quick and simple to make and can provide excellent finishing touches to food both in terms of taste and appearance. The herb butters, whether speckled or worked to smooth greens, are usually served with grilled meats and fish. Neat pats of the butter should be placed on the food at the last minute so that it is just beginning to melt as the food comes to the table.

Many of the butters can be used to finish various white and fish sauces. The butter helps to accentuate flavour, as well as enriching and adding colour to the sauce.

For the sake of convenience, this section also includes Beurre Noir which is prepared hot at the last moment, with certain additions, and is used as a sauce.

Beurre d'Ail

*B*lanch 200 g (7 oz) peeled cloves of garlic for several minutes in boiling water, then drain well and pound to a paste. Mix with 250 g (9 oz) softened butter, pass through a fine sieve and reserve for use. This may be used to finish sauces and soups or cut into decorative shapes to garnish cold hors d'oeuvre.

MAKES 450 G (1 LB)

Beurre d'Anchois

*F*inely pound 100 g (4 oz) rinsed and dried anchovy fillets then mix with 250 g (9 oz) softened butter. Pass through a fine sieve. Cover with greaseproof paper and refrigerate until required.

Uses

Chilled pats or melted Beurre d'Anchois can be served with shallow fried or grilled fish accompanied with sprigs of bright green parsley and lemon wedges. Beurre d'Anchois may also be added to other fish sauces, in small quantities, to strengthen their flavour. Using a small rose nozzle, Beurre d'Anchois may be piped on to fish or egg hors d'oeuvre as decoration. It is also delicious spread on hot toast. The '*Mirabeau*' garnish for grilled meat requires 125 g ($4\frac{1}{2}$ oz) Beurre d'Anchois, together with 20 thin strips of anchovy fillet arranged trellis fashion on the chosen meat, 10 stoned olives, and a border of blanched tarragon leaves. The '*à la Niçoise*' fish garnish requires 250 g (9 oz) tomato flesh, sautéed in butter with a touch of garlic and a pinch of chopped tarragon added at the last moment, 10 anchovy fillets, 10 black olives, 1 tablespoon capers, 25 g (1 oz) Beurre d'Anchois and slices of peeled and depipped lemon.

MAKES 350 G (12 OZ)

Beurre d'Amandes

150 g (5 oz) freshly shelled and blanched sweet almonds
a few drops water
250 g (9 oz) butter, softened

Pound the almonds with the water to a fine smooth paste. Work in the butter and mix thoroughly. Pass through a very fine sieve. Cover with greaseproof paper and refrigerate until the butter is required.

Uses

This nut butter can be used to finish certain cream soups such as chicken or delicately flavoured vegetable soups. It may also be added at the last moment to white sauces, most usually Sauce Béchamel, page 30, or Sauce Velouté, page 28. This and other butters may be shaped into a cylinder by placing the butter in a sausage shape across a sheet of greaseproof paper. Bring half of the paper back over the butter, then slide a palette knife firmly up the paper towards the butter. This will help shape the cylinder cleanly, expelling any trapped air. Roll the butter up in the paper and chill. Pats of the butter may then be cut from this and used to garnish hors d'oeuvre.

Variations

Substitute shelled, skinned, roasted hazelnuts for the almonds to make ***Beurre d'Aveline*** or ***Beurre de Noisette***. 40 g (1½ oz) of this butter can be added to 300 ml (½ pint) Sauce Hollandaise, page 66, to make ***Sauce Noisette*** which is suitable for serving with poached salmon and trout. Make ***Beurre de Pistache*** by using shelled, freshly peeled pistachios instead of almonds and ***Beurre de Noix*** by using shelled, dried, peeled walnuts. These variations all have similar uses to Beurre d'Amandes.

MAKES 400 G (14 OZ)

Beurre Chivry

B lanch and refresh 100 g (4 oz) mixed fresh parsley, chervil, tarragon, chives and very young salad burnet. Squeeze dry and pound together with 25 g (1 oz) blanched chopped shallot. Work in 120 g ($4\frac{1}{2}$ oz) softened butter and pass through a fine sieve. This is also known as **Beurre Ravigote** and **Beurre Vert**, and can be served with grilled fish, used to colour white sauces a pale green colour, or used to garnish cold hors d'oeuvre.

MAKES 200 G (7 OZ)

Beurre Colorant Rouge

R emove any of the remaining flesh and particles from inside and outside of any shellfish shells, such as those of lobster, crayfish and prawns. Dry them in a slow oven, then pound them until fine. Add and mix in an equal weight of butter and place in a *bain-marie*. Allow the butter to melt slowly, stirring frequently. Pass through muslin into a basin of ice-cold water. When the butter has solidified, place in a clean cloth and squeeze to remove the water.

This can be used to colour and flavour shellfish soups and sauces where necessary, and gives a much better result than artificial colouring. **Beurre de Paprika** may be used as a more neutral colouring agent: to 250 g (9 oz) softened butter, add 2 teaspoons paprika previously cooked in butter with 1 tablespoon finely chopped onion. Mix thoroughly and pass through a fine sieve.

Beurre Colorant Vert

P ound 1 kg (2 lb) well washed and drained raw spinach, place it in a cloth and squeeze tightly to extract all the juice. Place the juice in a small pan in a *bain-marie* and allow the juice to coagulate. Tip on to a clean cloth, stretched taut over a bowl, and allow to drain well. Scrape the colouring substance from the cloth with a palette knife and mix it with twice its volume of butter. Sieve finely and keep cool until required.

This can be used in various soups and sauces to give a delicate natural green colour and is far more satisfactory than artificial green colouring. In making Sauce Chaud-froid au Vert-pré, page 60, use the spinach colouring substance before any butter is added to it.

Beurre d'Echalote

R oughly chop 120 g (4½ oz) shallot, blanch quickly and drain well. Squeeze dry in a cloth and pound until fine. Work in an equal quantity of softened butter, pass through a fine sieve, and keep covered with greaseproof paper until ready to use. Serve with grilled meat and fish.

MAKES 225 G (8 OZ)

Beurre d'Ecrevisse

175 g (6 oz) butter
25 g (1 oz) carrot, peeled and diced
25 g (1 oz) onion, peeled and diced
1 small sprig thyme
½ small bay leaf
a few parsley stalks
300 g (11 oz) crayfish, recently killed and gutted

*M*elt 25 g (1 oz) of the butter in a small pan and add the vegetables and herbs. Cook until they are light brown in colour, then add the crayfish. Continue to cook until the shells turn bright red.

Discard the vegetables and herbs, then shell the crayfish and pound the flesh and creamy parts until smooth. When cold, add the remaining butter, mix well and pass through a fine sieve. Cover with greaseproof paper and refrigerate until required.

The crayfish shells may be used to make Beurre Colorant Rouge, page 101.

Uses
This tasty butter is usually added to various white and fish sauces such as Sauces Béchamel, page 30, Mornay, page 68, Normande, page 72, and Velouté, page 28, for extra flavour. It can also be used to enrich and thicken small quantities of poaching liquor from fish to make a coating sauce.

Variations
Beurre de Crevette is made by pounding cooked shrimps with an equal quantity of butter then passing through a fine sieve. **Beurre de Homard** is made by pounding the creamy parts, eggs and coral of lobster with an equal amount of butter then passing through a fine sieve.

MAKES APPROXIMATELY 350 G (12 OZ)

Beurre d'Estragon

120 g (4½ oz) very fresh tarragon leaves
250 g (9 oz) butter, softened

B lanch the tarragon leaves for 2 minutes in boiling water, then drain and refresh. Squeeze dry and pound until fine, then mix well with the softened butter. Pass through a fine sieve. Cover with greaseproof paper and refrigerate until required.

Uses
Herb butters can be served melted or in pats with grilled meat and fish. For *Filets de Sole Déjazet*, coat some fillets of sole with flour, egg and fresh white breadcrumbs. Shape with a palette knife, then mark with a trellis pattern using the back of a knife. Shallow fry in clarified butter. Serve on a dish containing half-melted Beurre d'Estragon and garnish the fillets with blanched leaves of tarragon.

Various herb butters, including those mentioned below, can be used with shallow fried veal cutlets. Deglaze the pan with white wine and reduce until you have approximately 25 ml (1 fl oz), then add 1 tablespoon melted Glace de Viande, page 16, and 25 g (1 oz) of one of the herb butters. Use this to coat the veal cutlets before serving.

Variations
Prepare **Beurre de Ciboulette** and **Beurre de Basilic** in a similar fashion, replacing the tarragon with chives or sweet basil as appropriate.

MAKES APPROXIMATELY 350 G (12 OZ)

Beurre à la Maître d'Hôtel

250 g (9 oz) butter
1 generous tablespoon chopped fresh parsley
1 tablespoon lemon juice

*B*eat the butter until soft and very smooth, then work in the chopped parsley and lemon juice. Cover with greaseproof paper and refrigerate until required.

Uses
Of all the compound butters this is probably the best known. It is the classic accompaniment for dishes, usually grilled meats, garnished with bouquets of watercress and bouquets of straw potatoes (deep-fried *julienne* of potatoes). This is known as the '**Vert-pré**' garnish. Pats of the butter or melted Beurre à la Maître d'Hôtel can also be served with grilled, shallow-fried or deep-fried fish.

Variations
A variation particularly well suited for serving with grilled meat and fish is made by the addition of 1 tablespoon Dijon mustard to the recipe as given above.

Another butter suitable for serving with grilled fish and meat is **Beurre Colbert**: add $2\frac{1}{2}$ tablespoons melted Glace de Viande, page 16, and $2\frac{1}{2}$ tablespoons chopped fresh tarragon to the above recipe.

MAKES APPROXIMATELY 250 G (9 OZ)

Beurre Marchand de Vins

200 ml (7 fl oz) red wine
25 g (1 oz) shallot, peeled and finely chopped
salt
freshly ground or crushed pepper
1 tablespoon melted Glace de Viande, page 16
150 g (5 oz) butter
1 tablespoon lemon juice
1 tablespoon chopped fresh parsley

*P*our the wine into a small pan, add the chopped shallot and reduce by half. Season with a pinch each of salt and pepper, then add the melted Glace de Viande. Allow to cool. Beat the butter until soft and stir in the wine mixture, lemon juice and chopped parsley. Beat until smooth.

Uses
This soft butter is best made just before it is required and is particularly suitable for serving with grilled sirloin, fillet and rump steaks.

MAKES APPROXIMATELY 225 G (8 OZ)

Beurre de Montpellier

40–50 g (1½–2 oz) mixed leaves of fresh watercress, parsley,
chives, chervil and tarragon, in equal quantities
15 g (½ oz) spinach leaves
20 g (¾ oz) shallot, peeled and finely chopped
25 g (1 oz) gherkins
2 teaspoons capers, squeezed
½ clove garlic, peeled
4 anchovy fillets
375 g (13 oz) butter, softened
2 small hard-boiled egg yolks
1 raw egg yolk
100 ml (3½ fl oz) olive oil
salt
cayenne pepper

*B*lanch the watercress, herbs and spinach, then refresh and drain. Separately blanch the shallot, then drain and squeeze dry. Pound these all together with the gherkins, capers, garlic and anchovy fillets. Work in the softened butter, all the egg yolks and finally the oil, drop by drop. Pass through a fine sieve and whisk until soft and smooth. Finish by whisking in a pinch of salt and a point of cayenne pepper.

Uses
This light green, highly flavoured butter makes an ideal accompaniment for cold poached fish, either served in a sauceboat or used to coat the fish.

Variation
For decorative purposes, the cooked and raw yolks and the oil should be omitted. The butter is then spread evenly on to a tray and chilled before cutting out into various shapes with hors d'oeuvre cutters.

MAKES APPROXIMATELY 375 ML (13 FL OZ)

Beurre Noir

Cook the required amount of butter in a frying pan until brown in colour. Tilt the pan over the heat occasionally to ensure that the butter colours evenly, then pass through a fine strainer into a small saucepan. Allow to cool until lukewarm, then add a few drops of vinegar, previously reduced with a little coarsely ground pepper. When required, reheat the butter, without colouring further, and add a little coarsely chopped, fried parsley and a few capers.

This is served with dishes designated '*au Beurre Noir*', which include grilled fish such as skate, boiled salt cod and some egg and vegetable dishes.

Allow approximately 20 g ($\frac{3}{4}$ oz) of butter per person.

Beurres Printaniers

These butters are prepared using vegetables and are frequently employed in the finishing of soups and sauces. The vegetables are first cooked according to their particular nature and requirements, e.g. carrots and turnips are stewed in butter and Fonds Blanc, page 10, while green vegetables such as French beans, peas and asparagus tips are cooked in boiling salted water until just tender. The cooked, drained vegetables are then pounded with an equal weight of softened butter and passed through a fine sieve.

In some instances the butter may be replaced with an equivalent amount of good quality cream, which absorbs the flavour and aroma of the vegetable more thoroughly than does butter. These preparations are known as cullises.

GLOSSARY

bain-marie a shallow water bath or roasting tin containing hot water in which food can be gently cooked or kept warm.

beurre manié a mixture of one part flour to one-and-a-half or two parts soft butter mixed to a smooth paste, and used to thicken sauces towards the end of the cooking period. Add in small pieces, then re-boil, whisking well.

brunoise vegetables cut into very small, regular dice.

cordon a small amount of gravy or sauce poured in a thinnish line around an item of food on a serving dish.

emincés thin slices of cold cooked meat reheated in a suitable sauce and then garnished.

fines herbes a mixture of chopped fresh parsley, chervil, tarragon and chives.

julienne items of food cut into regular matchstick-sized strips.

mirepoix a mixture of carrot, onion, celery and unsmoked bacon cut into a brunoise (q.v.) and lightly browned in butter with a bay leaf and thyme.

poêlé a method of roasting which takes place in a closed container and uses butter as the cooking medium.

timbale deep round ovenproof dishes used for the serving of well-sauced dishes. Timbale cases can also be made by lining moulds with pastry dough or forcemeat.

INDEX